BASIC PRINCIPLES
OF CLASSICAL BALLET

RUSSIAN BALLET TECHNIQUE

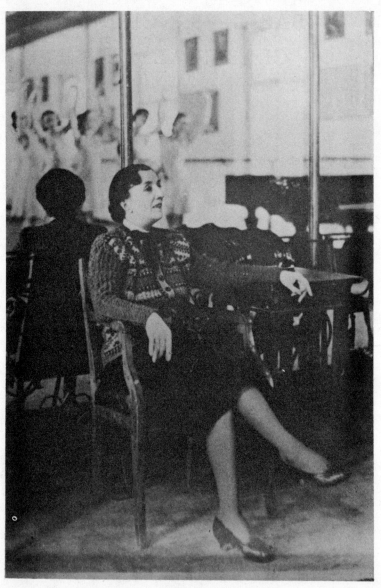

AGRIPPINA VAGANOVA

BASIC PRINCIPLES
OF CLASSICAL BALLET

RUSSIAN BALLET TECHNIQUE

by

AGRIPPINA VAGANOVA

Translated from the Russian by

ANATOLE CHUJOY

Incorporating all the material from the
Fourth Russian Edition

Including Vaganova's
"Sample Lesson With Musical Accompaniment"
translated by John Barker

DOVER PUBLICATIONS, INC.
NEW YORK

This Dover edition, first published in 1969, is an unabridged and unaltered republication of the second English edition published in 1953 by A. & C. Black, London. The *Introduction to the Fourth Russian Edition* and the *Supplement,* prepared and translated by Stanley Appelbaum, and the *Sample Lesson With Musical Accompaniment,* translated by John Barker, are taken from the fourth Russian edition. An *Index* has been added based on entries from the first edition published in 1946 by Kamin Dance Publishers, New York.

Standard Book Number: 486-22036-2
Library of Congress Catalog Card Number: 68-17402

Manufactured in the United States of America
Dover Publications, Inc.
180 Varick Street
New York, N.Y. 10014

INTRODUCTION TO THE
FOURTH RUSSIAN EDITION

AGRIPPINA VAGANOVA'S BOOK *Basic Principles of Classical Ballet* first appeared in 1934. Even then it was evident that the book's significance far exceeded the bounds of a teaching manual. The method expounded in it for teaching classical ballet represented a remarkable contribution to the theory and practice of the balletic art, a summation of the achievements of Soviet choreographic instruction.

Vaganova's system is the natural development and continuation of the traditions of the Russian school of ballet. The creative efforts of many Russian choreographers, instructors and dancers were directed toward the perfection of the technique and expressiveness of classical ballet. Many well-known foreign instructors also worked for the Russian stage. The skills that they imparted were assimilated creatively by the performers and were sometimes considerably altered in stage practice. The enormous experience amassed by those associated with Russian ballet was critically interpreted and systematized in the Soviet period, and became the innovative basis of the activity of Soviet ballet instructors. This grandiose work was headed by Agrippina Vaganova, a professor of choreography, a People's Artist of the Russian Soviet Federative Socialist Republic and an instructor in the Leningrad State Ballet School which now bears her name.

The book *Basic Principles of Classical Ballet* is known and prized by the entire choreographic world. Translated into English, German, Spanish, Polish, Czech, Hungarian and many other languages, it has crossed the borders of all countries where the art of ballet exists. It can be stated with certainty that the translations of this book have promoted the consolidation of the worldwide glory of Russian ballet no less than the guest appearances abroad of outstanding ballerinas—pupils of Vaganova—and the most prominent dance troupes of the country. Vaganova's experience is a guide to the authors of contemporary foreign manuals of classical ballet. All the more reason for the great popularity of her teaching system in our country. Three Russian-language editions of *Basic Principles of Classical Ballet* have proved to be insufficient to satisfy the needs of Soviet dancers, choreographers, dance instructors and a steadily growing army of participants in amateur ballet activities. In the last few years, with the broadening of the network of choreographic education and the appearance of new dance ensembles, the need for a fourth edition of Vaganova's book has become evident.

In the creative life of Agrippina Yakovlevna Vaganova (1879–1951) two periods can be clearly distinguished. The first of these, her stage career as a dancer, she usually recalled with bitterness. The second, her activity as an instructor after the Revolution, brought her worldwide recognition. And yet these periods are interconnected. It is precisely in her dissatisfaction with her artistic career that the sources of her subsequent achievements lie concealed. The pages of Vaganova's recently published memoirs[1] reveal the figure of a woman who was a persistent seeker from her very youth.

A brilliant dancer of the Maryinsky Theater, Vaganova had become famous as the "queen of variations" in ballets in which the leading roles were performed by Pavlova and Karsavina, Preobrajenska(ya) and Kshesinskaya (Kchessinska), but she received the title of ballerina only a year before her farewell benefit performance, and in 1916 she left the stage for good. She left deeply disappointed. . . . The causes of this were rooted not only in the atmosphere of routine prevalent on the Imperial stage. Extremely self-critical and demanding, Vaganova became aware of the inadequacies of her dance technique. "It was obvious that I was not progressing. And that was a terrible thing to realize. So then, I started to feel pangs of dissatisfaction both with myself and with the old system of teaching," she wrote in the rough draft of her memoirs.[2] Vaganova never lost an opportunity to learn from her older stage companions, but the principal factor was still her independent work, her search for a personal approach to ballet on the basis of a critical assimilation of the experience of her contemporaries.

Her first conclusions were drawn from a comparison of two systems of ballet teaching that served the Russian stage at the end of the nineteenth century under the conventional appellations of French and Italian schools. The representatives of the so-called

[1] A. Ya. Vaganova, pub. by "Iskusstvo," Moscow–Leningrad, 1958.
[2] The A. Ya. Vaganova Archives in the collections of the Leningrad State Theater Museum, No. КП 10371/329, A. Ya. Vaganova, "My Journey," p. 2.

French school were the well-known Russian ballet instructors Nicholas (Nikolai) Legat and Paul (Pavel) Gerdt. Vaganova took lessons from them in the Ballet School or in the theater. By way of Gerdt's teacher Johansson, under whom Vaganova also studied, the traditions of the "noble" classical ballet could be traced back to the Danish instructor and choreographer August Bournonville, and even further: to the illustrious French choreographers and dancers of the eighteenth century, including Jean-Georges Noverre. This was the origin of the "French" school of ballet.

The traditional lesson of the French school at the close of the nineteenth century cultivated soft and graceful, but unnecessarily artificial and decorative, movements. Vaganova was later to recall, not without irony, the reproofs she heard from her instructors: "Lightfooted! Lightfooted! Be coquettish!" Deliberately emphasizing the archaic traits of this dance manner, Vaganova writes of its saccharine sweetness, the flaccidity of its poses—the arms with softly sagging or affectedly elevated elbows and "elegantly" outspread fingers. In short, the disregard for the full use of the energy of the arms and body, and the tranquil and measured manner of conducting the exercises restricted balletic virtuosity.

The Italian school differed sharply from this old manner of instruction and performance. This school reached its acme in the last quarter of the nineteenth century. It was represented in the classroom by Enrico Cecchetti and on the stage by the guest performers Pierina Legnani, Carlotta Brianza, Antonietta Dell'-Era and many others. The virtuosity of the Italian ballerinas, who sought to astonish their audience with the most difficult steps—for example, the thirty-two consecutive fouettés, demonstrated for the first time—was not received in Russia without reservations. In the brilliant technique of the Italian ballerinas the people concerned with Russian ballet often found a lack of poetry and content.

In the years when Enrico Cecchetti worked for the St. Petersburg stage, the authority of the Italian school rose significantly. Particularly convincing were the swift successes of his Russian pupils. The advantages of the Italian execution became evident; it cultivated reliable aplomb (steadiness), dynamic turns and the strength and endurance of the toes. Another thing that attracted attention was that the conducting of the lesson was well thought out: Cecchetti had a fixed study plan for every day in the week, whereas the majority of instructors worked without a clear program. The immense usefulness of Cecchetti's lessons is attested by many Russian ballerinas, including Anna Pavlova, who for many years periodically traveled to Milan in order to study with the renowned teacher. Vaganova, too, speaks of Cecchetti with profound respect. She calls Cecchetti's activity "an event that played a tremendous role in the history of our instruction, and likewise in the history of Russian ballet."[1] But the merits of the Italian school did not prevent Vaganova from discerning in it tendencies alien to Russian ballet: an excessive angularity of movement, a strained use of the arms—now stretched out too much, now sharply bent at the elbows—and a harsh manner of tucking the legs under in jumps.

However, it was not only Vaganova who noticed this. Just as still earlier the prominent Russian ballerinas and dancers had creatively converted the principles of the French school into their own national style, so the Italian school was also substantially transformed in Russia. "Cecchetti's pupils smoothed out the rough spots in his method and the Italian pattern of steps (for example, bending the legs under in jumps), and the indubitable advantages of the Italian influence did not leave any one of the talented representatives and pupils of the French school indifferent," states Vaganova.

The famous stars of the Russian ballet, Anna Pavlova, Tamara Karsavina, Olga Preobrajenskaya and their predecessors, possessed a strongly national manner of dancing: a poetic spirituality, a purely Russian "cantilena" of dance movements, a wealth of expressive plastic nuances. But the Russian school, in the broad sense of the term, was not yet consolidated in its teaching practice. And this became the concern of Vaganova's life. Recalling the lessons of one of her beloved instructors, Yekaterina Vazem, who had been able to develop in her pupils strength and softness in plié; profiting by Preobrajenskaya's advice and elucidations of the Italian method; keeping an attentive eye on the choreographic activity of the young Fokine, who had achieved in his ballets a rare spirituality in dancing, a freshness in the poses and natural and poetic arm movements—Vaganova gradually selected the most distinctive features of the Russian manner of dancing. She became more and more conscious of her desire to investigate the "science of ballet," to find effective means of training classical ballerinas.

The second period of Vaganova's creative activity began right after the Revolution. In 1918 she began to teach in the private

[1] The A. Ya. Vaganova Archives, "My Journey," p. 2.

Russian School of Ballet directed by the ballet critic and fervent advocate of classical ballet, Akim Volynsky, but three years later she moved to the State Ballet School.

Vaganova's teaching method took shape during the twenties, a difficult time for Soviet ballet, when the classical heritage was exposed to the onslaught of pseudo-innovators. The formalistic "left-wing" press called ballet a hothouse art, wholly conditioned by the feudal way of life and doomed to destruction under the new circumstances. "And the ballerina's tarlatan costume and the rest of that high wisdom—all that dates from Montgolfier and his balloon."[1] "Classical art, rooted in the galanterie of the age of the kings Louis . . . is organically alien to our age."[2] Similar categorical declarations dotted the pages of newspapers and magazines. After the classical repertoire, classical dance—the arch-principle of ballet—was subjected to attacks. In place of the system of classical training of dancers, the apologists of the "new" art suggested "theaphysical training," athletic gymnastics, "eccentric" dance, "mechanical" dance, "acrobatic" dance. . . .

If the theater suffered considerably from biased criticism, which urged it onto the path of formalistic experiments, the position of the State Ballet School was no better. The school was charged with deliberate conservatism, backwardness, creative impotence; the critics demanded its reform "from top to bottom." And during this period, within the walls of the Leningrad State Ballet School an instructional system rigorously tested in practice was being developed, a system later made known to the whole world as that of Agrippina Vaganova.

Naturally, the results were not immediately noticed, although as early as 1923 Vaganova turned out the excellent pupils Olga Mungalova and Nina Mlodzinskaya, and in 1924 Natalia Kamkova and Elena Tangieva-Birzniek. The following year, 1925, is registered in the annals of Soviet ballet as the year of the unprecedented triumph of Marina Semyonova (Semenova) and of her instructor. Contemporary viewers were astonished by the virtuosity of the seventeen-year-old dancer, the rich orchestration of her movements, the impetuosity of her tours, the unusual expressiveness of her melodious arms. Semyonova was recognized as a consummate ballerina, but the essence of her talent was at first misunderstood. The critics saw in her "the flower of old-fashioned art," an exceptional, but accidental, phenomenon,

---

[1] *Zhizn' iskusstva* (Art Life), 1925, No. 25, pp. 9 and 10.
[2] *Zhizn' iskusstva* (Art Life), 1927, No. 6, p. 6.

whereas she was really the harbinger of the new Soviet choreographic school.

The following year Vaganova turned out Olga Jordan, then Galina Ulanova and Tatiana Vecheslova (1928), then Natalia Dudinskaya and Feya Balabina (1931). The critics noted the strongly individual character of the talent of the young ballerinas. But at the same time they found in Ulanova's dancing "much of Semyonova's style ... grace, the same exceptional plasticity and a sort of captivating modesty in her gestures."[1] It was evident that these were the traits of a school that had been definitely formulated. There still appeared here and there in the press the former demands for the "renewal of the theater, starting with the Ballet School," but in the meantime a significant balletic generation came into being, trained by Soviet instructors and above all by Agrippina Vaganova.

Vaganova's system was consolidated in close connection with theatrical practice. If in the twenties the people concerned with Soviet ballet were defending the classical heritage against pseudo-innovators, in the thirties the chief task was the creation of a contemporary repertoire. From 1931 to 1937 Vaganova headed the ballet ensemble of the Academic Theater of Opera and Ballet. In that period the ballets *Flames of Paris, The Fountain of Bakhchisarai, Lost Illusions* and *Partisans' Days* were created. The new versions, staged by Vaganova, of the ballets *Swan Lake* (1933) and *Esmeralda* (1935) corresponded to the general orientation of the Soviet choreographers' quest in the thirties for a sharpening of ideological conflict, for the efficacy of ballet, for veracity in the communication of human feelings.

In the new ballets the performance style of the dancers was strengthened and polished. The principles of this style were developed by the Soviet choreographic school, which can be called Vaganova's. Starting in the thirties, the artistic homogeneity of the Leningrad ballet troupe became obvious. "It is not necessary to be a special connoisseur in the field of ballet to observe in the performances of our theater and of everyone, from the girls in the corps de ballet to the leading ballerinas, something they have in common in their manner of execution. A single style, a single dance 'handwriting,' which manifests itself most clearly in the harmonious plasticity of movement and the expressiveness of the arms, in the responsive suppleness and at the same time the iron aplomb of the body, in the noble and natural placement of

[1] *Rabochii i teatr* (The Worker and the Theater), 1926, No. 9, p. 13.

the head—and these are the distinctive traits of the 'Vaganova school' "—so writes Natalia Dudinskaya in her reminiscences of her instructor.[1] Decidedly rejecting the excessive decorativeness and posing that had occupied a large place in the choreography of the past, Vaganova sought from her pupils emotional expressiveness, strictness of form and a resolute, energetic manner of performance. The dancing of Vaganova's pupils corresponded to the very essence of Soviet ballet as an art of great meaning, lofty lyricism and heroic spirit.

Vaganova's method also exerted influence on the development of male dancing. Male dancers who never studied directly with her acquired the "iron" aplomb that was purely Vaganova's, the ability to find support in their body, to gain *force* (a reserve of strength) with their arms for turns and jumps. In the State Ballet Schools of Moscow and Leningrad, Vaganova's experience was acknowledged and grasped by other instructors, and her pupils gradually disseminated this experience throughout the country. Finally, the publication of the book *Basic Principles of Classical Ballet* made Vaganova's method the property of the entire Soviet ballet theater.

New features in this significant method were the rigorous planning of the teaching process, the considerable complexity of the exercises, directed at the creation of a virtuoso technique, but mainly the aspiration to teach dancers a conscious approach to every movement. Vaganova's pupils not only thoroughly mastered a step, but they were also able to explain how to perform it correctly and what its purpose was. Making them write down the separate combinations, suggesting that they find the reasons for the unsuccessful execution of a step, Vaganova developed their understanding of the correct coordination of movements.

Vaganova considered the firm training of the trunk of the body to be the major prerequisite of free bodily control in dancing. From the first pliés, which she recommends learning compulsorily in the first position—more difficult for beginners, but in turn important for the strengthening of the body—her efforts were directed toward the creation of aplomb. Later on, aplomb becomes the foundation for tours and complicated jumps in the allegro.

In her book Vaganova frequently emphasizes the fact that movements must be begun "from the body," since dancing "from

[1] N. Dudinskaya, "Unforgettable Lessons," in *Agrippina Yakovlevna Vaganova,* "Iskusstvo," 1958, p. 191.

the body" ensures reliable support and artistic coloration of the step. The special attention she gave to épaulement (the turning of the shoulders and the body) is attested by the fact that it was impossible at her lessons to see two pas executed in succession with the same attitude of the body. Having developed in her pupils the necessary stability and suppleness, she then boldly introduced into the exercises various forms of fouetté, renversé and other movements based on the turning of the body.

The correct training of the arms was also an object of Vaganova's unremitting concern. Naturally, there is no need to speak about the feet, since every school of classical ballet strives above all else for the development of turn-out, long strides and strong toes. Vaganova paid no less attention to the arms. According to her method, the arms must not only crown the artistic picture of the dancer, must not only be expressive, light and "melodious," but must also actively aid the movement in high jumps and especially in tours, which are sometimes performed without a preparatory "springboard" push-off—here the *force* depends exclusively on the ability to control the arms. It was no accident that the technique of all sorts of turns was improved by Vaganova.

In short, Vaganova's system aimed at teaching pupils to "dance with their whole body," to acquire harmony of movements, to widen their expressive range.

In the book the movements are grouped by fundamental types. In a work of this sort there was only a limited possibility of dwelling at length on the conducting of the lesson. In connection with this, it is worthwhile to point out some of the book's notable features. All pupils remark on the unusual fullness of Vaganova's lessons, the complexity and swiftness of pace of the exercises, the diversity of the choreographic combinations. If Vaganova considered a great number of repetitions of movements helpful and necessary for beginners, in order better to develop the elasticity of the ligaments, in her advanced classes she would vary the lesson infinitely. Being opposed to the mechanical learning of steps, Vaganova set them forth in varied combinations which she had always thought out in advance—she did not believe in improvisation by an instructor during a lesson. This kind of lesson kept her pupils in a state of rapt and eager attention, increased their activity and was of greatest use to them. Developing the creative initiative of her pupils, Vaganova often requested them to devise a short adagio or allegro from the material that had been covered.

Never remaining content with what she had already accomplished, as the years went on Vaganova made her lessons richer and more intricate. The artistic innovations of choreographer-producers did not escape her notice. She unhesitatingly introduced all new movements into her lessons in order to prepare the aspiring artists and young students for working in contemporary productions.

Vaganova wrote in one of her last articles:

"Pupils who have not seen me for a long time find an improvement and progress in my teaching.

What is the cause of this? Diligent attention to new types of productions.

Look at life all around; everything is growing, everything is moving forward. Therefore I recommend . . . keeping in touch with life and with art."

That is the important precept Vaganova left to her followers.

Now Vaganova's instructional method has become the foremost and the basic method of the entire Soviet choreographic school. It is being creatively developed by Vaganova's followers, who work in various ballet academies in the nation.

The efforts of a number of Soviet instructors are perfecting the methodology of ballet teaching. While Vaganova was still living, her associates at the Leningrad State Ballet School, Alexander Shiryaev, Alexander Bocharov and Andrei Lopukhov, worked out, for the first time in the history of balletic art, a method for character ballet, expounding it in the book *Basic Principles of Character Ballet* (published by "Iskusstvo," 1939). Now Leningrad instructors are preparing fundamental studies on the methodology of teaching classical ballet in the younger classes of ballet schools, on the pas de deux and so on. New methodological materials are being published in the *Bulletin* of the Moscow State Ballet School.

Vaganova herself by no means regarded her instructional system as immutable or fixed once and for all. Guided by her vast experience, Vaganova's pupils are enriching and emending this instructional system in their creative practice. Thus, a number of ballet classes now give successful exercises on the high, not the low, half-toes. In the last few years, the expansion of cultural ties has created the possibility of international exchange of creative experience in the field of choreographic instruction, as in other fields. The people concerned with Soviet ballet have not failed to notice the achievements of foreign dancers in the area of ballet technique, particularly in tours and virtuoso beats. Special attention is now being paid to these areas of ballet exercise.

Perfecting the methodology of ballet teaching, enriching the lexicon and emotional expressiveness of movements, the Soviet instructors, followers of Vaganova, are striving to make their choreographic school correspond to the current level of Soviet balletic art, augmenting the glory of this art.

Vaganova's book *Basic Principles of Classical Ballet* is now being reprinted on the basis of the third edition. The only thing omitted is a brief article of the author, "In Lieu of a Foreword"; the characteristics of the various instructional systems discussed in the article are already inadequate for the present day.

Striving to emphasize the features of the Russian school of ballet, Vaganova often compares it in her book with the French and Italian schools. These concepts cannot be applied to the current foreign ballets, although in individual cases the methods described by Vaganova still occur in choreographic practice. The simplest approach in reprinting the book would have been to omit these passages, but since the citing of examples from the French and Italian exercises helps the author to elucidate the nuances of movement, they have been retained as having a practical significance.

The fourth edition of *Basic Principles of Classical Ballet* was prepared while Vaganova was still living. A few emendations were introduced by the author; these have been taken into account in the present edition.[1]

V. CHISTYAKOVA

[1] A copy of the third edition of Vaganova's book with her emendations for a fourth edition is preserved in the Leningrad State Theater Museum, No. КП 10372/3.

For her assistance in my research I wish to thank L. A. Rozhdestvenskaya.

INTRODUCTION TO THE
SECOND ENGLISH EDITION

MADAME VAGANOVA has written a work that should be found on every dancer's bookshelf. As a distinguished professor and custodian of a great tradition, she has produced a comprehensive and unaffected text book of real value. Her outlook is so refreshingly broadminded and professional; there is a real sense of proportion towards that vexed question—traditional schools and their technical differences. What a lesson there is in her balanced judgement, her unbiased approach. A life of study and devotion to the ballet has given her a rich store of knowledge, and a real insight into her pupils' requirements, and with the wisdom of those who know, she shows that there is no way of unduly hurrying the leisurely development of the perfect dancer.

That one might argue a point or two within these pages is of no real significance or importance. The brow that covers the mind behind this work is broad enough to demand our universal tolerance and blessing; and the mind behind that brow has acquired the only form of freedom of outlook that matters; that which springs naturally from an assimilated knowledge that is the result of a great discipline.

In this short foreword I salute the Russian School of Ballet, and pay a little of the homage that is due to a great professor.

NINETTE DE VALOIS

AUTHOR'S PREFACE*

A FEW EXPLANATORY remarks about the method of description used in this book.

First of all about the French terms accepted for the various conceptions of classical ballet. As I have long since indicated in discussions on this subject, the French terminology is unavoidable because of its international character and universal acceptance. It is similar to the use of Latin in medicine and English in sports.

In describing the forms of classical ballet I used an order which, in my opinion, is convenient for those who wish to acquaint themselves with classical ballet as a whole. For this reason I grouped the descriptions of battements, jumps, turns, etc., in an order which does not follow the order of their teaching, but which offers a simple systematization of the entire material in this book. In each chapter the description of steps is carried from the simplest form to the most complex and difficult, so that even the non-professional reader may be able to find easily the information in which he is interested.

Those who wish to acquaint themselves with the order of exercises given during a lesson, with the combinations of steps, etc., will find this information in the chapter on the construction of a lesson and in the examples furnished with the various descriptions.

In the descriptions of the various steps, I say that the right foot is front, or that the right foot begins a movement without modifying the description each time by saying that the movement may also be begun by the left foot, or that the left foot may be in front. I do this for the sake of conciseness of description, for convenience. The left foot may and should be used as often as the right one.

I also try not to repeat the description of a once-described method of execution, if that method was included in the description of another step. The reader, coming across an unknown term, must look up this term in the index and read its description in the indicated place.

In the majority of cases I give the description of a step in its full form, in the centre of the floor, with arms; if in the illustra-

*See Supplement, note 1.

3

tion that accompanies the description the step is shown at the barre, the arm movements can be easily added from the description in the text.

To indicate the degree of the turn of the body, or the specific direction of a movement, I use the diagram reproduced here. On it: a—indicates the position of the pupil on the floor, 1—the middle of the footlight line, 2—the corner in front and to the right of the pupil, 3—the middle of the right side, etc.

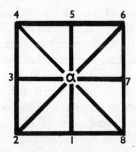

1. Floor plan. The spectator is at point 1; the dancer at point *a*

Our school accepts the method of measuring the position of the arms and legs used in anatomy. We indicate in degrees the angles formed by the arms and legs in relation to the vertical axis of the body. But it must be understood that we speak in general terms when we say that a leg is raised to 45°, 90°, 135°, because the angle formed by the leg and the body depends on the individual structure of the dancer. In other words, a 90° angle does not always equal a mathematical 90°; it is a conventional description of the horizontal position of the leg with the toe on the level of the hip.

I could not decide whether to use the precise anatomical and bio-mechanical terminology in defining the parts of the body, legs and arms. In the end I gave up this thought because I knew that these scientific definitions are much too seldom used among dancers. Although it may be clumsy writing, I prefer to say each time: "the upper part of the leg from the hip to the knee", "the lower part of the leg, from the knee to the toe", etc. It may not be very literary, but I thus avoid the possibility of a misunderstanding.*

*See Supplement, note 2.

CONTENTS

NOTE ON ILLUSTRATIONS

Where two sets of figures are found, the arabic numerals indicate the different stages of the movement illustrated, while the written numbers denote the musical counts.

BASIC PRINCIPLES
OF CLASSICAL BALLET

RUSSIAN BALLET TECHNIQUE

CONSTRUCTION OF LESSON

THE STUDY of any pas in classical ballet is approached gradually from its rough, schematic form to the expressive dance. The same gradation exists also in the mastering of the whole art of the dance, from its first steps to the finished dance on the stage.

The lesson does not unfold immediately as a whole but develops through exercises at the barre and in the centre to adagio and allegro. Children who begin to study at the start do exercises at the barre and in the centre only in dry form, without any variations.

Then simple combinations at the barre are brought in and repeated in the centre. Basic poses are studied. Further, easy adagio is added, without complicated combinations, so that it serves only to acquire stability.

Complexity is brought in by combinations of movements, into which we introduce work with the arms. In this manner we gradually come to the combined, complicated adagio. All movements which I describe below in their most elementary form are done on half-toe.

Finally, jumps are brought into the combinations of adagio, which lead the pupil to ultimate perfection.

In adagio the pupil masters the basic poses, turns of the body and the head.

Adagio begins with the easiest movements. With time, it gets more and more complicated and varied. In the last grades, difficulties are introduced one after another. Pupils must be well prepared in the preceding grades to perform these complicated combinations—they must master the firmness of the body and its stability—so that when they meet still greater difficulties they do not lose their self-control.

A complicated adagio develops agility and mobility of the body. When, later in allegro, we face big jumps, we will not have to waste time on mastery of the body.

I want to dwell on allegro and stress its particular importance. Allegro is the foundation of the science of the dance, its intricacy and the bond of future perfection. The dance as a whole is built on allegro.

I do not consider adagio sufficiently revealing. The dancer is assisted here by the support of her partner, by the dramatic or lyric situation, etc. It is true that a number of difficulties, even virtuosities, are now introduced into adagio, but they depend to a great extent on the skill of the partner. But to come out on the stage and make an impression in a variation is something else: here is where the subtleties and finish of your dance will be shown.

And not only variations, but the majority of dances, both solo and group, are built on allegro; all valses, all codas are allegro. It is vital.

And if we look back, we see that until now everything was just a preparation for the dance. Only when we reach allegro do we beging to study the dance. And this is where the whole wisdom of classical dancing is revealed.

In a burst of joy children dance and jump, but their dances and jumps are only instinctive manifestations of joy. In order to elevate these manifestations to the heights of an art, of a style, we must give it a definite form, and this process begins with the study of allegro.

When the legs of the pupil are correctly placed, when they have acquired a turn-out, when the ball of the foot has been developed and strengthened, when the foot has gained elasticity and the muscles have toughened—then may we approach the study of allegro.

We begin with jumps which are done by a rebound of both feet off the floor, changement de pieds and échappé. To make them easier they are done in the beginning at the barre, facing it and holding on with both hands.

The next jump to be done is assemblé, rather complicated in structure. This sequence has deep and important reasons.

Assemblé forces the dancer to employ all muscles from the very start. It is not easy for the beginner to master it. Every moment of the movement has to be controlled in performing this pas. This eliminates every possibility of muscular looseness.

The pupil who learns to do assemblé properly not only masters this step but also acquires a foundation for the performance of other allegro steps. They will appear much easier to the pupil, but in spite of it she will not be tempted to do them loosely. The correct setting of the body, the full control of it, once mastered from the first pas, becomes a habit.

It would be infinitely easier to begin to teach balancé, for example. But how can we instill in the pupil the correct manner of holding the body, or controlling the muscles? Because of the easiness of this step, the legs loosen involuntarily, and the pupil does not learn to turn-out as in assemblé. The difficulties found in assemblé lead directly to our goal.

After assemblé we may pass over to glissade, jeté, pas de basque, balancé. The latter, I repeat, should not be introduced until the muscles are fully developed in the basic jumps, and the jump is given its proper foundation.

Having learned how to do jeté we pass over to jumps on one foot, with the other foot remaining sur le cou-de-pied after the jump, and to sissonne ouverte to various sides. At the same time we may study pas de bourrée for, although this step is done without leaving the floor, it requires very steadily placed feet. At this period of development of the pupil we may begin to give her simple dances.

In the highest grades we study the most difficult sustained jumps and leaps, for example saut de basque. The most difficult of them, the cabriole, completes the study of allegro.

I dwell longer on allegro because it is the foundation on which the dance as a whole is based.

In the higher grades, when it becomes necessary to make the lessons more and more complicated, all steps may be done en tournant. Beginning with simple battement tendu and ending with the most intricate adagio and allegro steps, everything is done en tournant, affording the developed and strong muscles harder work.

I cannot give a rigid plan for the construction of lessons. This is the realm where the decisive part is played by the experience and sensibility of the teacher. It requires absolute individualization.

This is also true of the work of dancers: their daily exercises and preparation for performances. We must approach exercises as we approach the treatment of an illness. We get orders from a doctor, but the individual knows best how the orders should be carried out.

Professional ailments of the legs are frequent among dancers; they must vary the order of exercises so as to bring the affected spot into working condition with the least discomfort.

Here I think it necessary to say that I fully subscribe to the opinion prevalent among many dancers about the usefulness of work during the summer heat. I urge my pupils not to suspend their daily exercises for the summer. Great improvement can be made during the summer months because our system is ready for

13

work. One does not have to lose time in warming up, the legs are warm, more susceptible, and one can get more benefit from every effort.

From the first year of study and until the end of the career, the daily exercises of the pupil and dancer consist of the same steps. True, at the end of the first year the pupil is not yet doing all the exercises, but even the beginner goes through the movements which will later form part of the full exercises of the dancer.

With the exception of the first year, during which the steps come in a different order, the following succession of exercises should be adhered to. The exercises begin with plié in five positions.

It is not an accident or a silly tradition that we work through pliés in the order of positions, i.e., beginning with the 1st position. It is easier to do plié in the 2nd position, if you do it carelessly. But it is easier to teach a correct plié in the 1st position.

When you stand in the 1st position your balance is less firm. You have to make a certain effort to keep to the vertical axis around which the balance of the dancer is built. This forces control of the muscles, not to project the buttocks when squatting. The whole body is better concentrated, the position is correct; there is a foundation for any plié.

All this is much more difficult to achieve in the 2nd position. It is easy to get the pupils used to loosened muscles, while we are striving toward a composed body at the straightening of the legs for an elementary demi-plié.

After plié come battements tendus. The purpose of battements tendus is to produce, from the very lowest grades, a dependable and strong turn-out, so that later, during jumps, the feet will form themselves into a precise, correct 5th position.

It would be too late to offer suggestions and corrections during the study of jumps. The teacher should demand from the very beginning that the feet form the 5th position accurately and solidly. Only then will the correct 5th position become part and parcel of the dancer.

After battements tendus come ronds de jambe par terre, battements fondus, battements frappés, ronds de jambe en l'air, petits battements, développés, grands battements jetés.

All these steps may be combined and elaborated depending on the class, the approach of the teacher, and the method he employs elop the ligaments, muscles and joints. I only want to point out that in the lower grades the pupil's time should not be taken up with a variety of combinations.

There is nothing bad about the exercises being tedious in their monotony, although this monotony can be broken by doing the movements in different time, four-four and two-four, so that the pupils do not do them mechanically but follow the music.

In these classes a foundation is laid for the development of the muscles, the elasticity of the ligaments; a basis is instilled for the elementary movements.

All this is accomplished by systematic repetitions of the same movement a great number of times in succession. For example, it is better to do one step eight times in succession than two or four combinations of steps for eight bars. Few, scattered movements will not achieve the aim. The teacher must be absolutely certain that the pupil has mastered the movement, that it becomes part of her and that it will be done correctly in any combination, before he may complicate the lesson without harm to the pupil.

If this is not done, the teacher will get the pupil to understand the movement, but her legs will remain loose, and not a single step will be mastered to the finish.

In a word, if we force on the pupils too much posing instead of technical work on the movements, their development will progress very slowly.

In the intermediate grades combinations are allowed, but they should be gone into very carefully. It should be remembered that these intermediate grades must form the great power which the dancer needs, and which allows her, in the higher grades, to concentrate all her attention on the development of the dance art.

Barre exercises in the higher grades seem to be short in time, but this is an erroneous impression. The same exercises are done every day in the higher grades as in the lower grades. But because of a developed technique they are done in fast tempo and they take, therefore, less time. But they still give the muscles the necessary elasticity.

The exercises in the centre consist of the same steps as at the barre; adagio and allegro being added toward the end.*

---

*See Supplement, note 3.

BASIC CONCEPTIONS OF CLASSICAL BALLET

POSITIONS OF THE FEET

THE FIVE fundamental positions of the feet are universally known.

There are five of them because, for turned-out legs, a sixth cannot be found, from which it would be easy and convenient to move. There are reversed positions, with the toe pointing in, intermediate positions, between one position and another; but comfortable positions are limited to five only.

2. Positions of the feet

In the first position, the balls of both feet are completely turned out, the heels touch and the feet form a single straight line. In the second position the balls of both feet are also on one line, but there is a distance of one foot between the heels. In the third position one foot is in front of the other, heels touching the middle of the other foot. The fourth position is similar to the third, the feet being parallel and one short step apart. In the fifth position both feet touch so that the toe of one foot reaches the heel of the other.

PLIÉ

Plié is done in five positions. It is begun with a half-movement, demi-plié, and only after this is fully mastered, the full movement, grand plié, is introduced.

Plié is inherent in all dance movements. It is to be found in every dance pas, and therefore particular attention should be paid to it during exercises. If a dancer lacks plié, her performance is dry, coarse and devoid of plasticity. But if the lack of plié is noticed in a pupil, the shortcoming can be corrected to a certain extent. *How many*

People who are naturally endowed with a talent for the dance have a very pliant Achilles' tendon, and the leg easily forms an acute angle with the foot. Others have an Achilles' tendon that bends with great difficulty.

In such cases it is necessary to begin a struggle with nature, and here we must exercise great caution and consideration. Therefore, if the feet of a pupil who finds it hard to plié should begin to hurt, especially the ligaments, it is best to refrain for the time being from working on her plié, and return to this work later and do it gradually and carefully.

In the study of plié the following rules should be complied with, not forgetting at the same time to distribute the weight of the body equally on both feet. The study of plié should begin at the barre, holding on to it with one hand.

1st position		2nd position		3rd position
	a		b	

3. Grand plié: a—correct way; b—incorrect way

At the beginning, demi-plié should be carefully mastered. It is done without lifting the heel from the floor. The teacher should pay particular attention to this fact, as keeping the heel on the floor develops the tendons and ligaments of the ankle-joint.

In demi-plié, as well as in grand plié, it is very important to force the knees wide open, i.e. to turn out the whole leg. Particular attention should be paid to the upper part from the hip to the knee. The knee should always be bent in the direction of the toes. That is so that the knee is over the foot.

In grand plié, keep the heels on the floor as long as possible. When it becomes impossible to stretch the tendons any longer, lift the heels off the floor softly and gradually, never with a pull. The heels should not be kept off the floor for any length of time; begin to raise yourself and lower the heels without any delay.

one   two

three   four

4. Grand plié in 1st position

In the 2nd position, the heels should not be lifted off the floor, because in this position one can squat deeply without lifting the heels. The feet should be one foot apart. This short distance is most helpful in the development of the pliancy of the legs. In this plié the buttocks should not protrude, as this will give an incorrect form to the movement and will not develop the turn-out of the hips, which is the aim of this plié.

Upon reaching the extreme point of the plié in the down movement, the pupil should not remain there even for a moment, but should immediately begin to straighten up. If a pupil remains "sitting" in a plié, she not only does not improve the energy of the muscular drive and the elasticity of the whole leg, but, on the contrary, the legs—the levers of the jumps—acquire a sluggishness. Dancers call it "setting oneself on one's feet".

It is equally dangerous for some pupils to do too great a number of pliés at one time. This, too, can "set one on one's feet".

The lowering to the extreme point of the plié should last as long as the rising and should progress gradually.

When plié is done in the centre the following movements of the arms are added:

Before beginning the plié the arms are opened in the 2nd position, through the preparatory and 1st position. At the beginning of the plié the wrists are thrown up and the arms are lowered. When the plié reaches its extreme point the hands are down. Upon rising, the arms are opened through the 1st into the 2nd position as gradually as the legs move, without delay at any point and without haste. Such is the movement of the arms for all positions (except the 4th) when plié is done en face.* When the pupils get acquainted with the directions of épaulement, croisé and effacé, they do plié in 4th position holding the arms in the following positions: if the right foot is front, the left arm is in 1st position and the right arm in 2nd. The arms should be left in these positions during the entire plié whether the body is effacé or croisé. If the left foot is front, the position of the arms changes accordingly.

Croisé   Effacé

5. Demi-plié in 4th position and full plié in 5th position

Later on, when the pupil learns to use her arms, this plié may be done also with port de bras.

ÉPAULEMENT (HEAD AND SHOULDERS)

Épaulement is the first suggestion of future artistry of classical dancing which is brought into beginners' and children's exercises.

The study begins with the movements of the legs. The pupil stands en face, directly facing the teacher, until she gets used to doing the exercises holding the body still. Then some play of the body may be introduced and a hint of future artistic colour added.

En face is the natural direction for the 1st and 2nd positions and generally they remain so. But the 3rd and 4th positions are done with a turn of the shoulder: if the right foot is forward, the right shoulder is turned forward and the head is turned to the right.

The 4th position permits a dual turn. If the position is taken

20   *See Supplement, note 4.

croisé, the right shoulder is forward and the head to the right, if it is taken effacé, the right foot is forward, but the left shoulder is turned forward and the head to the left.

In this manner the basic characteristic of classical ballet is introduced from the very beginning, since classical ballet is built on croisé and effacé. It is from croisé and effacé that the richness of its forms is drawn, and it could never blossom out so luxuriously were it confined to the tedious and monotonous directions en face.

CONCEPTIONS OF CROISÉ AND EFFACÉ

Speaking of épaulement, we arrive at the two basic positions of classical ballet and point out their indispensability for the development of diversity and completeness in the forms of the dance. I shall now discuss the basic types of croisé and effacé.

CROISÉ

The fundamental characteristic of croisé is the crossing of legs. The croisé position can be forward and backward.

Croisé forward: stand on left foot, right leg open forward with the toes pointed, front of body turned toward point 8, head to the right, left arm lifted in 3rd position and the right one taken to the side in 2nd position. This is the basic pose of croisé forward, but the arms and head may be arranged in various ways and combinations.

Suppose you lifted your right arm and took the left one into 2nd position. To finish the design, you may incline your head forward so as to look under your right arm; or lift your eyes toward the left arm, in which case the head must be thrown back a little.

With this variation of the direction of your eyes, the facial expression will change involuntarily. In the previous poses, the inclined head draws together the features of the face; in this pose,

| 6. Croisé derrière | Croisé devant | Effacé devant | Effacé derrière |

the lifted eyes and the thrown-back head smooth the features—
the expression becomes more strict and spiritual.

It is very desirable to introduce these changes of facial expression as early as possible, so as not to have later on an expression which is once and for all petrified, or an eternal frozen smile.

Croisé backward: stand on right foot with the same turn of the body and head, left leg extended behind with toes pointed. In the basic pose of croisé forward the arm which was lifted contrasted with the extended leg; here the arm is lifted which corresponds with the extended leg; i.e. left arm lifted, right one to the side, head to the right.

Here, too, the arms and head may be arranged in various combinations. For example, right arm lifted, left one to the side, body slightly forward, head inclined so as to look under right arm. One arm may be lifted upward, the other one bent into 1st position, etc.

EFFACÉ

In this position, in contrast with croisé, the legs are open.

Effacé forward: stand on left foot, right one open forward with toes pointed, body facing point 2; head to the left, left arm in 3rd position, right arm open in 2nd position, body thrown back.

This is the basic pose. But you may bend the body forward and look under the left arm. There are also other possible combinations; for example, the wrists may be turned outward, etc.

Effacé backward: stand on right foot, left one backward with toes pointed in direction of point 6; the same direction for head, arms and body. But the body is slightly bent forward, and the pose assumes a hint of flight. Other combinations are also possible.

TURNS. EN DEHORS AND EN DEDANS

EN DEHORS

The conception en dehors defines rotary movements directed outward. Anyone studying the dance should master this conception and its opposite—en dedans—from the very beginning. The elementary descriptions I give here are for the benefit of those who want to have a clear understanding of these terms.

Let us take the first example of en dehors with which the pupil will come in contact from the very beginning. This is rond de jambe par terre. There are no difficulties here, as the leg obviously moves outward, describing an arc forward passes the 2nd position and back.

It is much more difficult to understand rond de jambe en l'air en dehors. The beginner is led astray by the fact that the leg extended in the 2nd position moves in the beginning of the movement in a half-circle seemingly inward, going through the rear half of the circle.

I have succeeded in explaining the direction of rond de jambe en l'air to pupils who could not understand it in the following manner.

I ask them mentally to transfer rond de jambe en l'air to the floor. If the leg in all parts of the circle goes in the same direction as in rond de jambe par terre en dehors we have a rond de jambe en l'air en dehors and vice versa. Then the pupil understands easily that en l'air she finishes with an outward movement, while par terre she begins with an outward movement, but in both cases it is the front arc of the circle which is en dehors.

As to en dehors in turns around one's own vertical axis, the most elementary explanation is the most comprehensive. You turn en dehors when you turn *away* from the leg on which you stand: i.e. if you stand on the left leg and turn to the right, the movement will be en dehors, and vice versa.

EN DEDANS

En dedans defines rotary movements directed inward.

For rond de jambe the explanation is analogous to en dehors, but the directions are changed accordingly. In turns, the movements will be *toward* the leg on which you stand: i.e. if you stand on the left leg the turn is to the left and vice versa.

En dehors   En dedans   En dehors   En dedans
from right foot   from left foot

7. Turns

If these basic conceptions of en dehors and dedans are mastered in the elementary movements, it will be easy to understand them

23

in the more complicated cases, because they will always include the element either of rond de jambe or turns.

The conception en dehors also defines the turned-out position of the leg accepted in classical ballet. People who know nothing about classical ballet tell all sorts of false and nonsensical things about the turn-out. Therefore I shall explain the origin of the turn-out in detail, borrowing some terms from anatomy.

The turn-out is an anatomical necessity for every theatrical dance, which embraces the entire volume of movements conceivable for the legs, and which cannot be accomplished without a turn-out.

The turn-out is the faculty of turning out the knee to a much greater extent than is made possible by nature. The foot turns outward together with the knee; this is a consequence and, to a certain degree, an auxiliary movement. The aim of the turn-out is to turn out the upper part of the leg, the hip-bone. The result of the turn-out is freedom of movement in the hip joint. The leg can be more easily extended and crossed with the other leg.

In the normal position, the movements of the legs are greatly limited by the build of the joint between the pelvis and the hip. As the leg is extended, the hip-neck meets the brim of the acetabulum and further movement is impossible. But if the leg is turned out en dehors, the big trochanter recedes, and the brim of the acetabulum meets the side flat-surface of the hip-neck. This allows the leg to be extended to an angle of 90° and even 135°.

The turn-out enlarges the field of action of the leg to the proportions of the obtuse cone which the leg describes in the grand rond de jambe.

This is the importance of training the legs of a classical dancer in strict en dehors. It is not an aesthetic conception but a professional necessity. The dancer without a turn-out is limited in her movements, while a classical dancer possessing a turn-out is in command of all conceivable richness of dance movements of the legs.

STABILITY—APLOMB

To master stability in the dance, to gain aplomb, is a matter of primary importance to every dancer.

Aplomb is perfected during the years of training and can be fully gained only at the end of study. Nevertheless, I think it necessary to include aplomb in the basic conceptions of classical ballet, because a correctly set body is the foundation of every step.

We begin to master stability at the barre. During the exercises the body must stand straight on the leg, so that the dancer may release the hand which holds the barre at any moment and not lose her balance. This serves as an introduction to the proper performance of the exercises in the centre.

The foot on the floor should not rest on the big toe, but the weight of the body should be distributed equally over the entire surface of the foot. A body which does not stand straight on the foot, but inclines toward the barre, will never gain aplomb and balance. As the work progresses, balance is practiced on the half-toe and on the toe.

8. Position of the body: a, b—correct; c, d—incorrect

When the exercises are done on half-toe in the centre, the proper position of the arms facilitates stability. If the arms do not follow the position which I indicate below, it is very difficult to preserve stability. Only when the dancer has mastered the control of her body to the extent where she can, standing on one leg, hold a single pose for some time, may it be said that she has fully developed her balance and poise.

This definite stability is achieved only when the dancer realizes and feels the colossal part that the back plays in aplomb. The stem of aplomb is the spine. The dancer should learn to feel and control her spine through observation of muscular sensations in the region of the back during various movements.

When you manage to get the feeling of it, and to connect it with the muscles in the regions of the waist, you will be able to perceive this stem of stability.

And then a dancer may undertake freely the most difficult parts of our art, for example, big jumps on one leg, for the performance of which the correct manner of holding the back is indispensable.

II

BATTEMENTS

THE WORD battement in the terminology of ballet means the extension of the leg and its return to the position from which it has been extended. In classical ballet the battement has been moulded into many forms. In describing these forms we shall familiarize ourselves with the substance of this movement.

BATTEMENTS TENDUS

This battement is the foundation of the entire technique. It was created by a genius who had penetrated into the very substance of the build and functions of the various ligaments of the leg.

A simple example from the everyday life of a dancer proves it fully. When a dancer, while dancing, slightly twists a leg and cannot step on her foot because of an uncomfortable feeling, she carefully begins to do battements tendus, and quickly regains working ability.

It is a custom to do battements tendus before a dance in order to warm up the legs. The legs not only get warmed up through this movement, but they also get into working condition; as our dancers say, *they are brought up* for the forthcoming activity, particularly in allegro.

When one observes that the legs of a dancer do not move properly, it is easy to guess that she has not been brought up by doing strict battements tendus at the proper time.

BATTEMENTS TENDUS SIMPLES

At the beginning of the study, this battement may be done from the 1st position, as this is less complicated. However, the same rules must be observed as in the battement from the 5th position, which is described below, only the foot, naturally, must return into 1st position.

Feet in the 5th position, right one in the front. Arms are open in 2nd position.* The weight of the entire body is on the left foot, right one free and not carrying any weight.

Right foot glides forward, without lifting the toe from the floor. The movement is begun by the whole extended foot. The heel is kept as much turned out as possible, which makes it feel as if

*See Supplement, note 5.

the movement is begun by the heel. Then the movement is continued by the toes.

9. Battement tendu simple

If the movement is done carelessly, one often notices that the foot, with the toes gliding on the floor, is lifted from the floor before the extreme point accessible to the pointed toes and extended arch is reached, and is then put back on the floor. This manner of execution hinders the mastery of this movement in its correct form.

The legs must be turned out fully (en dehors). At the moment the foot returns to its position, the heel should be turned out as carefully as possible, so as to get a perfect 5th position. The toe does not follow the movement passively, but, so to say, underlines its return to the position at the heel of the left foot. This gives an artistic finish to the movement.

The same movement is done to the side in 2nd position and back.

When the movement is done to the side in 2nd position, care should be exercised that the right foot continues the straight line of the turned-out left leg. To do that, the entire force of the movement, in returning to the 5th position, should be directed toward carrying forward the carefully turned-out heel. The toe is forcefully pressed back. Only through the most careful turning-out of the entire leg, from the upper part to the lower, can zig-zags be avoided. They are inevitable when the position of the leg is wrong.

When the movement is to the side, the foot returns to the 5th position, alternately front and back. In carrying the foot back, the knee and the upper part of the leg should be kept up, so that the knee is turned out fully and does not bend. The battement back is done with the foot which is at the back in the 5th position.

BATTEMENTS TENDUS JETÉS

Battements tendus jetés are the same as battements tendus simples, and are done from 5th position; after gliding along the floor, the leg is thrust out at 45° to the front, side or back. The accent is on the close in 5th position. The upper part of the leg, the hip, should not be raised too high.

The foot does not stop at the extreme point, but passes through the 5th position and continues the movement. The French name of this battement—*jeté* (thrown)—explains the character of the movement.

This battement is of great educational importance, and it must be executed very precisely, observing the following rules:

During the forward movement, each time when the foot passes through the 5th position, the toe must touch the heel of the other foot.

The movement to the side should be approached with particular attention. The working leg must be turned out exceptionally well, as this plays the decisive part in the movement. In addition to that, the foot should not miss that point in the 2nd position, which the toe hits every time it is thrown, whether it passes the 5th position in front or in the back. The directions given for battements tendus simples should be observed.

In the movement to the back the upper part of the leg is again carefully kept up in a turned out position. The foot should move in such a manner that it is not seen from the front, and the knee does not bend. The pupil usually bends the knee voluntarily, to ease a difficult movement. In bringing the foot into the 5th position, the toe must in all cases hit the floor.

I consider it necessary to stress again the importance of the position of the upper part of the leg. The leg must be *taken away* to the back, the knee must not be dropped in and must be fully turned out. One must feel one's leg as a taut cord.

Battements tendus jetés should be taught after battements tendus simples are executed by the students with full perfection, and their legs are strengthened, and they can use them freely, without any strain.

BATTEMENTS TENDUS POUR BATTERIE

These battements are preparatory movements for beats, especially for men. The masculine build permits the execution of beats in a slightly different manner—with the upper part of the leg. A woman usually does beats with the calf of her leg, although she should try to do it the masculine way. But the build of a woman is different, the form of her hips and legs differs from those of a man, and they produce a different way of doing beats.

In class, these battements acquire the following form:

From the 5th position, the right foot opens into the 2nd, then the right calf beats the left leg in the front, is transferred back (without opening in the 2nd position) and from there opens into the 2nd position. At the moment of hitting the calf at the back, the right heel almost touches the floor.

Both legs must be extended energetically. One must feel that the beat is done with the calf forward, and the leg rebounds strongly, like a spring. Because of the extension of the leg in this manner, it cannot go farther than the 3rd position on its return. The leg never loses its position, i.e. it is fully turned out.

The movement is repeated, hitting first back and then front and opening in the 2nd position. The number of transfers of the foot may be increased, depending on the step for which this movement serves as a preparation.

For assemblé battu one transfer is sufficient; for entrechat two or more are necessary.

Speaking of the execution of all classic pas, it must be remembered that they are all done with the toes and arches extended (with the exception of those mentioned above). It must be understood that when we speak of extended toes we also mean extended arches, though we may not mention it every time. One cannot extend one's toes without also involving the arches in the movement.

GRANDS BATTEMENTS JETÉS*

These are done like battements tendus, but the leg continues the movement and is forcefully thrown out to an angle of 90°.

10. Grand battement jeté devant

*See Supplement, note 6.

The body should not make any involuntary movements, any tremblings which are the results of wrong efforts.

The body will remain quiet if the leg works independently, without involving other muscles in the movement. The inexperienced dancer tends to strain her shoulder, neck and arms. This is wrong. The hand which lies on the barre with the elbow lowered should not change its position. The barre should serve only as a point of support, and the dancer should not grasp it with force.

11. Grand battement jeté à la seconde

Only when the grand battement is done backward is it recommended to bend the body forward, because only in this position will the general line remain quiet and the leg work correctly.

In the exercise of the Italian school, the body is held straight also during the battement backward. But then the leg inevitably bends in the knee joint, and the entire line is restless and broken up.

In the beginners' class it is best not to demand an angle over 90° in this battement, so as not to spoil the performance of this movement for the sake of a cheap effect.

The teacher should hold back even those pupils whose individual build of the leg permits an angle of 135°. The finished dancer with an acquired self-assurance can choose any desired height.

GRANDS BATTEMENTS JETÉS POINTÉS

This battement begins with a grand battement jeté, but the foot does not return into the 5th position. The leg, extended at the knee and the instep, is lowered to the floor in the same position which it holds at the extreme point of a battement tendu simple.

Slightly touching this point with the toe, the foot is raised again and continues the movement, returning to the 5th position only in the last movement. The body, of course, remains in this battement as it was in the preceding.

30

12. Grand battement jeté pointé

GRANDS BATTEMENTS JETÉS BALANCÉS

This battement is done in exercises at the barre.

At the beginning the leg is taken back with the toes pointed. With a sliding movement the leg is thrown out through the 1st position forward to the angle of 90°, and due to the force of the throw, the body bends backward. Then the leg is thrown through the 1st position backward, the body bending forward. The result is a swinging movement forward and backward.

The body should bend evenly backward as much as forward, the back should remain straight and the shoulders on an even line.

Beginners should not be satisfied with bending the body only forward and trying to avoid the backward bend, though the latter is more difficult. If they do so, they deprive this exercise of its form and sense.

1 2 3

13. Grand battement jeté balancé

In the 2nd position battements jetés balancés may be used only in the centre, not at the barre, and it acquires a different form. The leg thrust into 2nd position is supplanted through 5th position by the other leg in 2nd position. As the legs are quickly interchanged, the body bends each time to the side of the supporting leg.

BATTEMENTS FRAPPÉS

The starting point of the right leg is in the 2nd position, with

31

the toes pointed. The right foot beats the left one sur le cou-de-pied front and returns to the 2nd position, hitting the floor with the pointed toe. The accent is in the 2nd position.

14. Battement frappé

Sur le cou-de-pied front is the position of one foot on the ankle of the other one. The sole, with the instep stretched out and the toes lowered, grasps the ankle. Sur le cou-de-pied back: the instep and toes in the same position, but the side of the heel and ankle are pressed against the standing foot from behind.*

When battement frappé is done back, the foot does not beat sur le cou-de-pied, but passes behind the ankle.

This form is used in the elementary study of the movement.

In the more advanced classes when battement frappé is done on the half-toe and the leg reaches the 2nd position in the air at 45° the same accent must be felt and directed to the same point of the 2nd position; the knee must be taut and springy, the contact with the left leg a short beat, the leg should rebound like a rubber ball. The upper part of the leg must be immobile and turned out; the leg must work without vibrating in the knee-joint.

BATTEMENTS DOUBLES FRAPPÉS

This is the same movement as battement frappé, but the foot does not beat the left leg in the front only once. It is transferred in a second passing beat sur le cou-de-pied back. From there it opens to the side, into the 2nd position. If the first beat is done back, then the second passing beat is done front.

PETITS BATTEMENTS SUR LE COU-DE-PIED

In the starting position the right foot is sur le cou-de-pied. It opens in the direction of the 2nd position, but only halfway, because the leg is not fully extended at the knee. Then it is trans-

*See Supplement, note 7.

ferred back, touching the left leg at the ankle, and opens again in the same manner, and returns front.

15. Petit battement sur le cou-de-pied

At the beginning of the study petits battements should be done without any accent.

At the moment of the transfer of the foot, attention must be paid that the instep is not shortened, that the sole does not bend.

The upper part of the leg from the knee to the hip must be firm, immobile, fully turned out and the lower part must do the movements freely. At the change to fast tempo, the opening of the leg gets shorter. But it must never fade and turn into a smear. Although the transfer of the foot from cou-de-pied front to the back is almost imperceptible to the eye, this movement should never lose its precision, and requires the same articulate execution as if done in slow tempo.

BATTEMENTS BATTUS

The starting-point is sur le cou-de-pied. From here the right foot does a number of short swift strokes on the heel of the left foot in the position sur le cou-de-pied front. The stroke should be done with the toe; the lower part of the leg should move freely.

16. Battement battu

This exercise should not be started before the leg is well developed. Usually, it is done only in the higher grades.

BATTEMENTS FONDUS

The right foot moves from the 5th position to sur le cou-de-pied, the left one simultaneously does a demi-plié, its knee turned out. Then the right leg opens forward with the toes pointed on the floor, the left one straightens out and extends in the knee-joint simultaneously with the right one. The right foot returns to sur le cou-de-pied, and the movement is repeated in the 2nd position and to the back. In the latter case the foot passes sur le cou-de-pied back.

Attention must be paid that in this battement the knee is not raised and the leg is not lifted. These two things are done only when the exercise is performed with the legs at an angle of 45° or 90°.

1 [1]   2   3

17. Battement fondu

In the grand and petit développé the legs should be turned out as carefully as in battements tendus. For example, in doing the

1 Current usage in the Soviet Union favors the pointed position sur le cou-de-pied.

34

movement back attention should be paid that the knee is not dropped, and that the upper part of the leg is well turned out.

This movement belongs to the category of more complicated exercises, because the leg on which the dancer stands also participates in the work, doing a plié simultaneously with the battement done by the other leg.

BATTEMENTS SOUTENUS

From the 5th position the right leg is taken out to the front, into the 2nd position, or to the back, the left leg simultaneously doing a plié. Then the left foot rises on the half-toe, the right leg is drawn to the left one, and both of them join in the 5th position on the half-toe.

18. Battement soutenu

From this point the movement is either repeated or is done to the other side. The leg that is being taken out should not be bent or raised too high (if the movement is done on the floor, and not at an angle of 45° or 90°).

BATTEMENTS DÉVELOPPÉS

From the 5th position the sole of the lifted right foot with toes pointed glides over the left leg up to the knee and opens in

19. Battement développé

the required direction, keeping the knee and the heel in a turned-out position.

If the lifted leg is not brought up to the knee, the movement looks careless. On reaching the extreme point (90°), the leg is lowered into the 5th position.

This movement is included in exercises in numerous variations:

1. With the extended leg being bent so that the toes touch the supporting knee, from which the extension is repeated;

2. With little movements of the extended leg, lowered slightly and re-lifted to 90°; these movements should be attempted with the toes only, so that the leg is not brought down too low, but just slightly swings;

3. The leg, extended forward, is drawn with a swift movement into the 2nd position and is brought to the front again, all in one count, with the accent on the forward movement; the same movement to the back; the same movement from the 2nd position forward and back.

4. With turns of the body. Do développé forward, make half a turn on the supporting leg into 2nd arabesque and return on the same leg, rotating the raised leg. In 2nd position: do développé in 2nd position, quickly change onto that foot, turning and opening other leg into 2nd position; do the whole figure again, and return to the initial position opening the leg in 2nd position. In changing the hands on the barre, grasp the barre with the free hand and change it simultaneously with the turn of the body.

Développé is a movement from adagio. Slow tempo is inherent in développé, and it should be performed with a retardation at the extreme point, especially in the lower grades.

The leg on which the dancer stands should be fully extended, like a taut string, the knee fully turned out. The arm which rests on the barre should be freely bent at the elbow. Particular attention must be paid to this when the forward movement is performed. Frequently the arm is strained, thus furnishing support for the leg. It is easier to stand in this manner, but the exercise under these conditions is useless.

Of the many forms of développé I shall describe the two most complicated.

BATTEMENTS DÉVELOPPÉS TOMBÉS

This battement, according to its type, belongs to small adagio. It is done mostly in the centre, but sometimes also at the barre. The movements are as follows:

Do a développé forward with the right leg, rise on half-toe, fall with the weight of the entire body into the deepest plié on the right foot; the left leg is extended and touches the floor with its toes only; transfer the weight back onto the left foot, while the right leg repeats the développé with a swift movement and

20. Battements développés tombés

returns to its open position, and the left rises onto half-toe.

This battement is done forward, as well as to side, back, and in the directions croisé, effacé, écarté.

In order to give this movement a wider form, I always advise my pupils to imagine that the leg has to be flung over some object.

5   4   3
four   three   two

2   1
one
21. Battements divisés en quarts en dehors

This does not let the dancer lower herself too soon during the fall of the body. The result is a very wide battement and the leg is flung very far.

BATTEMENTS DIVISÉS EN QUARTS

This exercise is done in the centre. It may be considered one of the first adagios. It consists of the following movements which may be done en dehors and en dedans:

From the 5th position, développé forward with the right leg, plié on the left leg; turn the body a quarter-turn to left on half-toe, rotating the right leg into the 2nd position. Bring the right leg in to touch the left knee, and, without lowering the leg into 5th position, repeat the movement from the beginning.

22. Battements divisés en quarts en dehors

The movement is done four times, each time turning one quarter-turn, thus making one full turn. The movement can be made more complex by making each turn a half-turn or even a full turn.*

Begin the same movement with développé back, and do all figures en dehors and en dedans.

38   *See Supplement, note 8.

III

ROTARY MOVEMENTS OF THE LEGS

RONDS DE JAMBE PAR TERRE

EN DEHORS. This movement begins from 1st position. The leg moves forward as in battement tendu; from here the toe describes an arc through 2nd position to a point opposite 1st position at the back. From this point the foot draws a straight line to the point from which it began the arc, passing through 1st position, with the heel lowered to the floor, and stretched-out knees.

En dedans. This movement is done in the opposite direction. The leg moves backward from 1st position and draws the same arc and straight line in the opposite direction, complying with the same rules. The movement is completed by placing the leg in 5th position forward.

When rond de jambe par terre is done in fast time, it is preceded by the following preparation:

From 5th position, move the right leg forward, doing a plié on the left leg, the arm going into 1st position. Draw the right leg into 2nd position, straightening the left knee and opening the arm into 2nd position.

If doing this movement in very fast time, when the foot cannot quite describe a full circle, in the movement en dehors the foot should reach its extreme point backward; and in the movement en dedans its extreme point forward.

The leg involuntarily goes astray and does exactly the opposite, i.e. en dehors it moves from 2nd position through 1st, forward; en dedans, from 2nd position through 1st, backward. This makes the movement too easy and does not provide the necessary work for the muscles.

RONDS DE JAMBE EN L'AIR

En dehors. From 5th position, the right leg is opened into 2nd position at 45°, the toes stretched out. From here the toe describes an oval (the long side in the direction of left to right), beginning with its backward arc. When the knee is bent and the toe is drawn in to the calf, but not under the knee, it should not reach beyond the calf of the left leg, either forward or backward. The hip-leg joint (pelvic arch) remains immobile, and thus the upper part of the leg, from the knee up, is also immobile.

23. Rond de jambe par terre and en l'air

En dedans. In the movement en dedans, the foot begins to describe the oval from its forward arc and, completing the movement, is lowered into 5th position front.

When rond de jambe en l'air is well mastered and the pupil begins to do it in faster time, strict attention should be paid to the retardation and fixation of the leg in 2nd position every time it passes this position.

As a preparation for this movement we may use temps relevé.

This is a very important movement playing a serious part in the further classical development of the body. It should be done in a particularly precise manner. Never let the leg shake in the knee joint, otherwise it will not get the full benefit from this exercise.

Properly executed, ronds de jambe en l'air make the upper part of the leg firm and strong and the lower part, from the knee to the toe, manageable in all rotary movements, in fouetté en tournant, for example. In this case it is particularly important, as any wrong motion of the leg may throw the dancer off balance. Besides, a well-developed lower leg which is manageable and pliable lends expressiveness to every movement of the leg in dance.

GRANDS RONDS DE JAMBE JETÉS

This exercise is done at the barre.

En dehors. In class this rond de jambe is usually preceded by rond de jambe par terre, which contains an impetus for the following forceful cast of the leg.

From 4th position back, the leg, is forcefully thrown forward, passes 1st position, flies up with toes pointed into a half-bent position at 45°, stretches out, describing a circle backward on the height of 90° by rotating the hip joint, and returns to 4th position. The circle should be made as wide as possible, the leg describing the widest arc it can.

24. Grand rond de jambe jeté

It should be done so that the leg works independently, without involving the body in the movement. This is possible when the muscles are fully developed and are subordinate to the will. In proper execution the body remains still, the tension of all the muscles supporting it is unnoticeable, and the leg works intensively from hip to toe.

En dedans. This movement is in the opposite direction.

The leg, passing from 4th position forward, through 1st position, should be thrown back into a half-bent position, firmly held at the thigh. This gives power and a wide girth to the whole circle described.

Grand rond de jambe jeté is a pure exercise movement. Expert dancers may occasionally allow themselves to begin their lesson with it: this movement at once brings the entire body into intensive work. But pupils and immature dancers should approach grand rond de jambe jeté through preliminary exercises, for the tension of the tendons and muscles of the hip is very great.

THE ARMS

POSITIONS OF THE ARMS

In my terminology of ballet I use only three positions of the arms; all other positions I consider variations of these initial three, and I feel that it is superfluous to introduce special names for them. And anyway, as soon as the teacher approaches a complicated exercise or a dance, the movements of the arms must be shown and not described.

The initial position of the arms is the preparatory position: the arms are dropped; the hands with palms inward are close to each other but not touching; the elbows are slightly rounded, so that the arm does not touch the body from the elbow to the shoulder and does not come in contact with it under the armpit.

preparatory position   1st position   2nd position   3rd position

25. Positions of the arms

The manner of holding the hands in the preparatory position, as well as in the subsequent positions, can be shown only in actual demonstrations. It is very difficult to describe. To a certain extent the accompanying illustration will help. I shall add the following explanation.

All fingers are grouped freely and they are soft in their joints; the thumb touches the middle finger; the wrist is not bent, but the hand continues the general curved line of the arm from the shoulder.

If at the beginning of an exercise the thumb is not pressed firmly on the third finger, all the fingers will become spread out, because the attention during the exercise will be transferred to the legs and the body. This grouping of the fingers may be modified as the pupil progresses.

First Position. The arms are raised in front of the body on a level with the diaphragm. They should be slightly bent, so that when they open into the 2nd position, they unbend and open to their full length. On raising the arm to the 1st position, it is held up from the shoulder to the elbow by the tension of the muscles in the upper part of the arm.

Second Position. The arms are opened at the side, very slightly rounded in the elbow. The elbow should be well held up by the same tension of the muscles of the upper part of the arm. The shoulders should not be drawn back or raised. The lower part of the arm, from the elbow to the wrist, is held on a level with the elbow. The hand, which due to this tension falls and appears to be hanging, should also be held up, so that it, too, takes part in the movement.

By holding up the arms in this position during the lesson, we develop them in the best manner for the dance. At the beginning the arm will look artificial; the actual result, however, will come later. The elbow will never drop, the arm will require no attention, it will be light, sensitive to every position of the body, alive, natural and highly expressive. In short, it will be fully developed.

Third Position. The arms are raised over the head, the elbows rounded; the palms are inward, close to each other but not touching. The dancer should be able to see them without raising her head.

The movement of lowering the arms from the 3rd position through the 2nd into the preparatory position should be done very simply: the arm will come into the correct position by itself upon reaching its final point.

The incorrect manner of some teachers who introduce an excessively sweet plasticity should be avoided. In bringing the arm into the 2nd position, they draw it slightly back and turn the hand palm downward. This breaks the line. The movement appears to be broken, unnecessarily complicated and sweetened.

I repeat, the hand will turn naturally when it is necessary. This artificial turn of the hand is a typical movement of dancers who call themselves plastic dancers.* Their meagre technique needs such adornments, because otherwise they will have nothing on which to build their "dances". We, in our school, do not need it.

Arabesques require a special position of the arms. The arm is extended in front, the hand placed palm downward. The elbow should not be extended too tightly, and the shoulder should not be pushed forward.

*See Supplement, note 9.   43

The French manner of bending the wrist upward obscures the expression of the whole figure and puts the accent on the arms; the audience looks at the arms and not at the general line. My manner is closer to the Italian, but the movement is freer, the fingers lie unrestrained, the hand is not so much stretched out.

PORT DE BRAS

Port de bras is the foundation of the great science of the use of arms in classical ballet. The arms, legs and body are developed separately through special exercises. But only the ability to find the proper position for her arms lends a finesse to the artistic expression of the dancer, and renders full harmony to her dance. The head gives it the finishing touch, adds beauty to the entire design. The look, the glance, the eyes, crown it all. The turn of the head, the direction of the eyes, play decisive roles in the expression of every arabesque, attitude—in fact, of all other poses.

Port de bras is the most difficult part of the dance, requiring the greatest amount of work and concentration. Perfect control over the arms is an immediate indication of a good school.

This is particularly difficult for those who are not naturally endowed with beautiful arms. They, more than anyone else, must watch their arms. Through a well-thought-out use of them, they can acquire beauty of line and movement. I have had pupils with naturally exquisite arms, who, through lack of knowledge of port de bras, had no freedom of movement. Only upon mastering port de bras did they begin to manage their arms.

It is necessary that the arms, from the preparatory position, be rounded so that the point of the elbow is not seen; otherwise the elbows will form angles which destroy the soft outline the arms must have. The hand must be on a level with the curve at the elbow; it must be held up and not be bent too much, otherwise the line will be broken.

At the present time there is a tendency toward undue stretching of the hands which gives a harsh, stiff line. The elbows must be held up and the fingers held in the indicated grouping. The thumb should not be stretched out.

Shoulders must be held down and left immobile. The positions of the arms and port de bras must seem spontaneous. Each movement of the arms (poses) must pass through 1st position. This principle must be applied both to dances on the floor and movements in the air.

As soon as one begins to study port de bras the execution of steps takes on a more artistic, polished appearance. The arm begins to "play".

If we do not require anything more of the hand than a correct position in relation to the entire arm, while the whole attention is centred on the development of the legs, the harm is not so great. Besides, to teach the arm to remain still, to be free and independent of the movement of the legs, is a very important stage in the development of a dancer.

With children and beginners the arms always attempt to imitate the movements of the legs, to share in the work; for instance, when doing a rond de jambe, the arm unconsciously describes a vague circle. But when the pupil manages to dissociate the movements of the arms and legs; when, with concentrated work of the legs, with sometimes terrific effort to achieve the desired movement, the pupil manages to leave the arm quiet, not participating in the movement—that already is a step forward.

Besides, in order to develop the arm, to bring it into an obedient and harmonious state, one needs infinitely less time than to develop the legs within the limits required for the classical dancer. The leg develops, strengthens, is disciplined by long continuous daily work. No matter how little time is left for the arms in comparison with the legs, they will get their necessary workout.

One recalls those plastic dancers who in several months develop quite bearable arms, while one cannot help but say that their bodies and legs are still in the most primitive condition.

Therefore when doing exercises designed to develop the legs, the hand may remain still, so long as it is held correctly. With port de bras the hand comes into play and gives the exercise its full colouring.

Here, too, begins the training for control of the head and its correct direction, as it is the head that determines every shading of movement. In port de bras the head participates all the time.

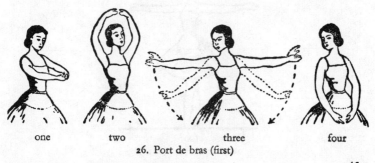

one   two   three   four

26. Port de bras (first)

Ports de bras are numerous and varied. There are no special names for the different forms. I shall cite several examples.

1. Stand in 5th position croisé, right foot in front. From the preparatory position the arms go into 1st position, are raised to 3rd position, open in 2nd position, and are lowered to their starting-point in the preparatory position.

one   two   three
27. Port de bras (second)

In order to lend this exercise the character it requires, in order, as we say in class, to "intake a breath with the arms" they must be used as follows:

When the arms arrive in 2nd position, open the hands, taking a deep, quiet, but not exaggerated breath (without lifting the shoulders!), turn the hands palms down, and as you exhale, bring

one   two   three

four
28. Port de bras (third)

them smoothly down, allowing the fingers to "trail" slightly behind, but without overemphasizing, and without too much break at the wrist.

The head bends to the left when the arms reach 1st position, the glance follows the hands; when the arms are in 3rd position, the head is straight; when the arms open, the head turns and inclines to the right. At all times the glance follows the hands. When the movement is finished, the head is straight once more.

2. Stand in 5th position croisé, right foot front. From the preparatory position the arms go to 1st position, then the left arm goes to 3rd, right arm to 2nd, then left arm to 2nd, right arm to 3rd. Then left arm is lowered to preparatory position, passes it and comes up to 1st, where it meets the descending right arm. From here the entire movement is repeated.

The head accompanies the movement in the following manner: When the arms are in 1st, glance at the hands inclining the head to the left; in the next position the head turns to the right; when the right arm is in 3rd position, the head inclines and turns to the left. At the conclusion of the movement the head is turned to the left.

3. Stand in 5th position croisé. Opening the arms into 2nd position (head to the right), "breathe" with them, as described in the first port de bras, and lower them into preparatory position, simultaneously bending the body and the head forward and keeping a straight spine all the time. Then begins the unbending which is done in the following manner: first, the body straightens out, i.e. rises to the initial position, during which the head and body are raised simultaneously with the arms; the arms move through 1st position into 3rd, then the body bends back as much as possible, but the head should not be thrown back, and the arms, according to the accepted rules, should be in front of the head and should not escape the eyes which are fixed on them; the body unbends, the whole figure straightens out, the arms open into 2nd position.

This port de bras may be done to a 4 beat rhythm: on *one*—bend the body forward, on *two*—straighten to initial position, on *three*—bend back, on *four*—return to initial position and open arms into 2nd position.

4. The following exercise belongs to the Italian school, but is now widely in use with us, and is applied to every exercise. However, in order to give it that stamp of artistic finish which is inherent in it (in spite of its seeming simplicity of form) great care

47

must be exercised in its proper execution. I shall endeavour to explain it in detail, although it is difficult to express in words the free, smooth flow of its interlacing parts.

Stand in 5th position croisé, right foot front. The arms go through 1st position, the left into 3rd, the right into 2nd position. Open the left arm into 2nd position, at the same time vigorously expanding the chest, tensing the back and arching the spine, bring left shoulder so far back as to see it well from the back in the mirror, and as you are thus turned to the left, the right shoulder will be in front. The head is turned to the right. In spite of the powerful turn of the body, the feet do not move. Then the right arm is moved into 1st position, where the left arm, rising from below, meets it. The body returns to starting position.

Now, the last of all details. When one arm is in 3rd, the other in 2nd position, the hands follow palms down, fingers extended as if cutting the air and meeting with some resistance, so that the wrist is slightly bent, hands trailing after arms.

When both arms reach 2nd position, and the body is completely turned as required, the arms relax at the elbow and even drop slightly; they are soft and effortless, like fins. This is caused by the tension of the arched back and gives this exercise the finished, non-classroom effect it should have.

| 1 | 2 | 3 | 4 | 5 |
| | one | two | three | four |

29. Port de bras (fourth)

5. This port de bras is usually done at the end of the lesson, when the body is well warmed up. It develops greater flexibility.

Stand in 5th position croisé, left arm lifted in 3rd position, right arm extended in 2nd; bend the body and head forward, without losing the straightness of the spine; left arm is lowered to 1st position, right arm, having passed through preparatory position, meets it (also in 1st position), the body bends back with a turn to the left; i.e. the left shoulder moves back. The arms move from 1st position thus: right arm rises to 3rd position, left extends into 2nd. Then the body returns to its starting position, right arm opens to 2nd position, left arm rises to 3rd.

6. Grand port de bras. Stand in croisé position, left foot extended behind (left arm already in 3rd position, right arm in 2nd). Plié on

30. Port de bras (fifth)

right foot sliding the left foot further behind; you may leave it either entirely on the floor, or raising the heel rest on the toes (the first way makes the body bend further and work harder). At the same time the body bends low forwards, with it goes the left arm without losing its position in 3rd position. Bending the body as far forward as possible, you should hold the spine straight, not allowing it to bunch over. In order not to lose this erectness, you have to hold the spine perfectly firm and straight, thus avoiding any hint of round shoulders. In the meantime the right arm is lowered and meets the left in 1st position without losing its position directly in front of the diaphragm. While you take as wide a 1st position as is possible within your particular structure, straighten the body, shift the weight on to left foot, raise the right arm into 3rd position and the left arm into 2nd (right arm always remains in front of the head!). Bend back, tensing well the muscles of the back. The head is thrown back over the left shoulder and the pose is analogous to the pose in the 3rd port de bras; i.e. the left shoulder is

31. Grand port de bras (sixth)

49

brought well back. Then the right arm opens into 2nd position, head turns right, body straightens to upright position, left arm moves to 3rd position, and with a plié you return to the starting croisé position.

This port de bras is often done in adagio as a preparation for a grande pirouette. In that case you do not bring the movement to its conclusion, but remain on the bent right leg in a widened 4th position, with right arm in 3rd and left arm in 2nd.

Then, for a pirouette en dehors the left arm is brought forward from 2nd position through 3rd into the pose préparation à la pirouette, while the right arm opens to 2nd position.

For a pirouette en dedans, having reached the same position of the arms, bring the rounded right arm into 1st position with a wide circling movement, leaving the left arm extended in 2nd position. That is the start of the pirouette.

The two last kinds of port de bras are very important in our training. A dancer who has mastered them can consider that she has found co-ordination of body, head and arms, and is well on the way to acquiring the play of the body.

I shall not cite any further examples of port de bras. They can be varied to infinity by combining their basic elements.

Just a few words about the work of the arms.

If, having done a développé, for example, you are standing with the leg extended in 2nd position at 90° and the arms are also in the 2nd position, you should lower the arms first, not moving the extended leg until the arms have begun to move. The lowering of the leg ends, however, simultaneously with the arms. This gives a firm control to the leg, and the entire movement acquires a calm, unhurried aspect.

When executing small movements allegro or adagio, i.e. in small poses, the arms should not be raised high. Only in large poses do the arms rise to full height. This has to be considered during small adagio and allegro, so that the play of the arms does not overshadow the movement of the feet.

EXAMPLES OF PARTICIPATION OF ARMS IN EXERCISES

When a complicated exercise combining various figures and steps is given, the arms are brought into the general movement, and play a significant part. For instance, there are many figures for développé and in all of them the arms take part in the movement.

Three ronds de jambe en l'air en dehors for 1½ beats with a rest on the fourth half-beat in plié on left foot and right foot in effacé forward on the floor; bending entire body, bring it and the arm to the extended foot. Open palm as if pointing to the toe. Then do three battements frappés for 1½ beats and rest on the fourth half-beat in 2nd position. Three ronds de jambe en l'air en dedans, rest in effacé back on the floor, plié on left foot. Bend body back, head over shoulder, glance at the toe. The arm is extended in front of the chest, palm down, hand outstretched and lifted. Finish with three battements frappés in the same tempo as in the first case, i.e. rest on the fourth half-beat in 2nd position.

Six petits battements for 3 beats of the bar, on the fourth beat fall in plié on right foot (changing the foot on which you were standing) and assume a small pose croisé with the right arm bent, left foot sur le cou-de-pied back; then change back to left foot and do four petits battements for 2 beats of the bar, and for 2 beats do a turn en dehors sur le cou-de-pied from préparation temps relevé.

All movements are repeated in the same tempo, but after the first six petits battements, fall on right foot in plié back, substituting left foot, which will come out sur le cou-de-pied front in a small pose croisé, right arm is half-open in 2nd position at 45°, then, after the subsequent four petits battements—temps relevé is done back and the turn—en dedans.

TEMPS LIÉ (IN THE CENTRE)

This is a widely used combination which starts in beginners' classes and gradually increases in difficulty.

The simplest temps lié is done as follows:

Stand in 5th position croisé, right foot front. Do a demi-plié, both arms in 1st position. Right foot glides forward into croisé, left remains in demi-plié. Shift weight on to right foot, point left foot behind. Bring left arm up, right arm out to side. Bring left foot from behind into 5th position en face in demi-plié, shifting left arm into 1st position, right arm remains in 2nd position. Slide the toe of right foot to side, leaving left in demi-plié, shift weight on to outstretched right leg (opening left arm into 2nd position), with pointed toe slide left leg into 5th position front in demi-plié. Drop arms into preparatory position. Repeat whole movement on left foot. The same movements are also done to the back.

I recommend beginners to study temps lié in $^4/_4$ time, doing the entire movement in two bars. First bar: *one*—demi-plié in 5th position; *two*—extend the toes forward in croisé, the passing plié falling between the second and third count; *three*—pose croisé behind; *four*—close in 5th position. Second bar: *one*—demi-plié in 5th position; *two*—leg carried out with extended toes into 2nd position; *three*—extend the toes of the left foot, changing weight to right leg; *four*—close in 5th position.

In advanced classes, temps lié can be done lifting the legs to 90° when moving forward and back, and into 2nd position. From 5th position demi-plié on the left foot, do a développé forward into croisé; change weight to right leg into attitude croisée behind, fall onto left leg into demi-plié, bringing it close to the right leg, which bends at the knee at 90°; développé with right leg into 2nd and step onto it on half-toe, lifting left leg into 2nd position at 90°, demi-plié on right leg, bending left into the right knee; bring it out forward and continue the movement to the other side. Arms are the same as in the movement on the floor.

Temps lié sauté consists of successive small sissonnes tombées, but it belongs to allegro.

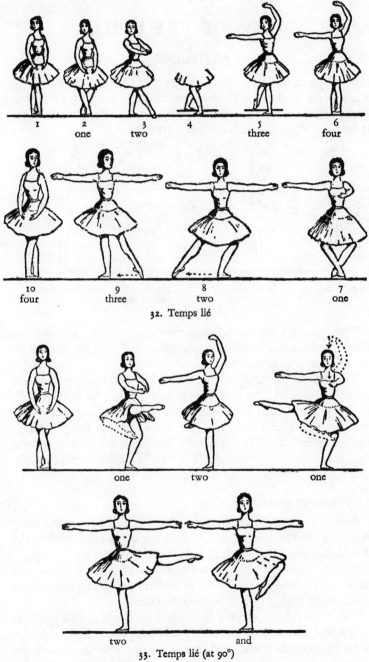

| I | 2 one | 3 two | 4 | 5 three | 6 four |

| 10 four | 9 three | 8 two | 7 one |

32. Temps lié

| | one | two | one |

| two | and |

33. Temps lié (at 90°)

V

POSES OF THE BODY

ATTITUDES

THE WORD attitude indicates a pose on one leg with the other lifted at an angle of 90° and carried back, bent at the knee. Therefore a pose with a développé forward cannot be called an attitude, as the leg in it is extended straight.

1	2	3	4
Attitude croisée	Développé croisé front	Développé effacé front	Attitude effacée

34.

These poses I do not call otherwise than développé croisé or effacé. In an attitude the corresponding arm and leg are lifted, the other arm is in 2nd position.

The knee of the lifted leg must be taken well back, and should never be dropped. The bent knee allows the body to bend as well. In doing turns, the movement is free and beautiful, whereas the straight leg in an arabesque does not allow the body to bend and impedes turns. To familiarize ourselves more closely with the attitude, we shall examine its execution by the French, Italian, and Russian schools, in croisé and effacé.

ATTITUDE CROISÉE

Attitude croisée in the French school is taken with the body bent toward the leg on which you stand, thereby raising the shoulder of the lifted arm much higher than the other.

In the Italian school the body is straight, the back is also straight, the design of the pose is determined by the turn of the head, or the lifting of one or the other arm.

This form of the attitude is incorrect because in this position of the body the knee is not sufficiently supported, and it appears to be hanging. If one should want to support the knee with the upper part of the leg, with the hip, the knee will move away from the body, and the resulting pose will be ugly.

My attitude croisée is as follows:

The shoulders are even, the body bent back, the back not straight but arched, the leg bent forcefully back. The head is turned definitely toward the shoulder. The body in atittude inevitably inclines toward the standing leg, but because of the tensed leg, and well-arched back, the shoulders are evened out, achieving the desired form. The arms may be changed, you may lift the one opposite the raised leg, changing the tilt of the body without spoiling the correctness of the pose. When the spine works properly one may play with the body at will.

ATTITUDE EFFACÉE

If in attitude croisée the leg must be bent in the knee, in attitude effacée it should be only half-bent, otherwise the resulting pose will not be beautiful.

<table>
<tr><td>1</td><td>2</td><td>3</td></tr>
<tr><td>French</td><td>Russian</td><td>Italian</td></tr>
</table>

35. Attitude effacée

The Italian attitude effacée conserves the straight back, nevertheless the body is distorted by being bent toward the bent leg. When doing a pirouette in this position, the pose is lost, either the knee hangs down involuntarily, or on the contrary, the knee rises and the toe hangs down.

My attitude approaches the French one. The body is directed toward the standing foot, slightly forward; the arms and the entire pose have an inclination in one direction, which lends this attitude an impression of flight. The difference between this attitude and the French one is the same as in attitude croisée. In spite of the direction of the body toward the standing foot, one shoulder is not higher than the other.

Such an attitude is extremely convenient for turns.

ARABESQUES

The arabesque is one of the basic poses in contemporary classical ballet.

If in attitude the leg is bent or half-bent, in arabesque it must always be fully extended. The forms of the arabesque are varied to infinity. The four principal arabesques accepted in our technique are the following:

1st Arabesque: (also called open, ouverte or allongée, but at present these terms are no longer in use).

The body rests on one leg. The other, extended and straight, is lifted from the ground to an angle of no less than 90°. The feet are in position effacé. The arm opposite to the lifted leg is extended forward, the other one is taken out to the side. The hands are held palms down, as if leaning on the air. The body is inclined forward. The head is in profile to the audience, as is the entire figure. The shoulders are level, as in all arabesques. The deciding factor in the arabesque is the back. Only by holding it well can one produce a beautiful line. In order to illustrate more fully the correct position, let us analyse the French and Italian arabesques, as well as ours.

36. 1st arabesque   2nd arabesque

The French arabesque takes the pose in a slipshod way, the back is not extended forward, not tensed; it just leans passively forward. The arm is artificially held in a 2nd position, which gives it a stiff, inexpressive look.

The Italian arabesque eliminates the laziness of the pose. The body is tensed but not inclined, the back remains upright, the arm is taken further back from the 2nd position.

I indicate the following arabesque:

56

The body is bent forward as much as the impulse forward is felt, the back is not relaxed, but strongly arched, tensed at the waist. The arm is brought out to the side only as far as is necessary for the comfort of all the strongly stretched muscles of the entire body, i.e. just a little behind the 2nd position.

2nd Arabesque: body and legs are the same as in 1st arabesque, but now the arm corresponding to the leg is extended forward. The other arm is brought back far enough to be seen behind the body. The head is turned to the audience.

3rd Arabesque: this arabesque faces the audience. The leg is croisé back at an angle of 90°. The body is bent forward, the back tensed. The arm corresponding to the extended leg is extended, the other one is taken out to the side. The face is turned toward this hand as if watching its movement.

37. 3rd arabesque   4th arabesque

4th Arabesque: the legs are in the same position as in the 3rd arabesque, but the arm opposite the extended leg is brought forward. The body is turned by the strong arching of the back. The other arm shows behind the back. This arabesque is half turned away from the audience, the head is turned toward the audience, emphasising its direction by the glance. The shoulders must be on the same level. The body must not lean forward. This is the most difficult of arabesques, and requires careful study of its form.

When we begin to do turns in arabesque, we begin to understand the relative value of the different arabesques, the French, Italian and ours.

In turns, the French arabesque does not allow us to develop the movement. The Italian arabesque invariably causes the knee to bend, breaking the line, which is habitually observed with Italian dancers. The arabesque I teach gives balance, energy in turning, and at the same time the extension of the entire pose and legs is not lost.

When doing a turn in arabesque, the arabesque must be clearly expressed. From the preparation (4th position croisé) one must, having pushed off with the heel of the front foot, take a definite arabesque, otherwise the turn will not be successful, the power will be lost. Being clearly conscious of this, one must "push off" into arabesque without counting on correcting the pose during the movement.

ÉCARTÉ

The pose écarté is done as follows:

Écarté back. Standing on right foot, bring out the left leg in a développé at an angle of 90° in the direction of point 6 in our diagram. The leg is strongly turned out from the hip. The entire pose is taken in one plane, diagonally toward the audience. The left arm is lifted into 3rd position, the right one into 2nd. The body must bend sideways toward the standing leg, but with a strong tensing of the back. The body must remain natural, but not so simple as to be inartistic. The head is turned to the right.

Écarté front. The leg is directed to point 8 in our diagram. The pose is proud, dignified. It is done in the same way as écarté back. The corresponding arm and leg are lifted, and the head is turned in the direction of the raised arm.

In both cases both arms may be raised.

38. Écarté back and écarté front

As a matter of fact, écarté is a développé in 2nd position, opened as widely as possible. In this pose one should pay special attention to the shoulders. In spite of the bend to the side the shoulders must not lose their line, and one shoulder must not be higher than the other.

VI

CONNECTING
& AUXILIARY MOVEMENTS

PAS DE BOURRÉE

In CLASSICAL ballet, to move from one spot to another, a dance step is used and not an ordinary walking one. One of the most widely used for this purpose is pas de bourrée.

Pas de bourrée has several variations, and it is done in all possible directions.

For a long time we used the soft, unemphasized pas de bourrée of the French school. With the strengthening influence of the Italian school in the nineteenth century, pas de bourrée changed in character. Now the foot is lifted sharply, the entire movement is defined in higher relief. I accepted this style after having tried it out in practice.

One must be careful that the foot leaves the ground smartly, both in the early stages of study on half-toe, and later on pointe.

Pas de bourrée is divided into two basic forms: with a change of feet, and without a change of feet. In the first instance, if you start with the right foot front, you will end with the left in front; in the second, the right foot remains in front.

PAS DE BOURRÉE WITH CHANGE OF FEET

To familiarize the pupil with pas de bourrée in the beginners' classes, the form with a change of feet is employed.

Stand croisé, left foot pointed behind (right sole entirely on the floor). Arms in preparatory position. Demi-plié on right leg. Step on left foot on half-toe, bringing it close behind the right foot; right foot pointed sur le cou-de-pied front and raised slightly on the left leg, step onto right foot on half-toe, toward 2nd position without moving too much from the spot; left foot sur le cou-de-pied front, as described above. Fall on left foot in demi-plié croisé. Right foot sur le cou-de-pied back. Arms take a small pose croisé. Repeat on the other foot, with the movement into the other direction.

Thus is executed pas de bourrée en dehors.

To execute pas de bourrée in the reverse direction, i.e. en dedans, begin in the pose croisé forward with the left foot pointed in front. Demi-plié on right foot (left foot—sur le cou-de-pied front), stand on left foot on half-toe, bringing it close to the right foot, raise right foot sur le cou-de-pied back, change to right foot on half-toe toward the 2nd position, not moving too much from the spot, left foot sur le cou-de-pied back, fall on left foot in demi-plié, in croisé, right foot sur le cou-de-pied front.

| 5 | 4 | 3 | 2 | 1 |
| three | two | one | | (up beat) |

39. Pas de bourrée (with change of feet)

With a series of such movements one may begin the study of pas de bourrée. Special care must be exercised that the feet are well lifted, that the toes are forcefully extended and pointed.

This teaches the sole of the foot to work in pas de bourrée, so that with increase in tempo, the sole will not be dead, but will move, if not exactly with the same sharpness as at the beginning of the study, at least it will participate in the movement.

PAS DE BOURRÉE WITHOUT CHANGE OF FEET

This pas de bourrée is done with the leg opening at the conclusion of the step and travelling to the side. When making the step to the side, the legs must not be held too far apart.

| 5 | 4 | 3 | 2 | 1 |
| three | two | one | | |

40. Pas de bourrée (without change of feet)

Stand in a pose croisé, left foot behind. Arms are in preparatory

60

position. Starting the movement, raise them the least bit and return to the same pose. Demi-plié on right leg, step on left foot on half-toe, right foot sur le cou-de-pied front (same as in preceding form of pas de bourrée). Step on right foot on half-toe, with movement to the right; left foot sur le cou-de-pied back. Fall on left foot in the demi-plié, right foot opens to 2nd position at an angle of 45°; the arms open in a low 2nd position.

To continue, step on right foot and repeat the same movement from the other foot to the left.

I repeat all these movements can be done in any direction: forward, back, in effacé, croisé, and écarté.

If you do pas de bourrée without change of feet in écarté, then at the movement to the right, when you stop, the right leg will be in écarté forward, and when moving in the opposite direction, to the left, the left leg will open in écarté back.

PAS DE BOURRÉE DESSUS—DESSOUS

In translation *dessus* means *over*, and the leg that is opened at the beginning of the movement goes forward first, replacing the other leg. *Dessous* means *under*, and the leg that is opened at the beginning of the movement goes behind, replacing the other leg. One may add, that in the first case the leg, as it were, goes over the other leg, and in this manner sur le cou-de-pied is always at the back of the stepping foot. In the second case, it goes under the other leg, and sur le cou-de-pied is always in front of the stepping foot.

Pas de bourrée dessus-dessous, as well as all other forms of pas de bourrée is taught at the beginning on half-toe.

1. *Dessus.* Stand in 5th position, right foot front. Arms in preparatory position. Demi-plié on right leg, open left leg to 2nd position at an angle of 45°, and step on it on half-toe, bringing it in front of the right leg;[1] the right rises at back sur le cou-de-pied, as in the preceding cases; the arms slowly open to a low 2nd position toward the end of the movement. Step on to right foot on half-toe, bringing it in front of the left; the left rises at the back sur le cou-de-pied (the same way). Fall on left leg in demi-plié; the right opens to 2nd position at 45°. The entire movement is done to the right.

[1] Special attention must be paid not to bring the foot forward in a half-circle. It must cut a straight line from 2nd to 5th position. By exercising this you will avoid sloppy execution in the future. In doing pas de bourrée en tournant with this detail, the pupil will involuntarily learn to control her back, which will then turn not abruptly, but with the correct slow speed.

41. Pas de bourrée dessus sur les pointes

42. Pas de bourrée dessous sur les pointes

The arms gradually join in the preparatory position, and open to a low 2nd position at the end of the movement.

2. *Dessous.* 5th position; demi-plié on left foot opening right leg to 2nd position and step on right foot on half-toe, left foot sur le cou-de-pied front. Step on left foot on half-toe behind the right foot, right foot sur le cou-de-pied front (the same way). Fall on right foot in demi-plié, left leg opens to 2nd position at 45°. Repeat entire movement to the left. Arms are moving as in the preceding example.

When first studying pas de bourrée the accent is made on the concluding plié. Eventually, however, the movement changes into an unaccented form, one pas smoothly following the other.

PAS DE BOURRÉE EN TOURNANT

In the dance this movement is often joined with another, serving as a preparation for it.

All described types of pas de bourrée can be done en tournant. As an example we shall analyze the following case:

Pas de bourrée en dedans. Stand in 5th position, right foot front. Demi-plié on right leg opening the left leg into 2nd position at 45°. While stepping on the left foot on half-toe, do a half-turn to the

| 5 | 4 | 3 | 2 | 1 |
| three | two | | one | |

43. Pas de bourrée en tournant en dedans

right, the right foot slides sur le cou-de-pied front. Finish the turn on right foot on half-toe, left foot sur le cou-de-pied back. Fall on left foot into plié, right foot sur le cou-de-pied front.

From this movement you can continue pas de bourrée en dehors in the following manner:

Demi-plié on left leg, open right leg into 2nd position at 45°, stepping on right foot on half-toe, do a half-turn to the right; left foot slides back sur le cou-de-pied. Complete the turn on left foot, right foot sur le cou-de-pied front, and fall on right foot in plié, opening left leg into 2nd position at 45°.

| 1 | 2 | 3 | 4 | 5 |
| | one | | two | three |

44. Pas de bourrée en tournant en dehors

The arms open at the beginning of the step into 2nd position at half-height, close into preparatory position during pas de bourrée, and open into any position required, depending on the step to follow.

The head faces the spectator as long as possible, and then follows the turn of the body.

PAS COURU

When many pas de bourrée are done consecutively, we get pas couru. Usually it is done in fast tempo. It is often used to gain momentum for big jumps, such as jeté, for instance, and is found abundantly in masculine dances.

It is also done frequently by women on pointes, moving in a straight line, diagonally, or in a circle around the entire stage.*

COUPÉ

This small intermediary temps is a movement facilitating the beginning of some other step. Coupé is done as a preparation, as an impetus for some other step, and is usually done on the final up-beat of a bar (pick-up).

Suppose you have to do pas ballonné forward, while you are standing on right foot in a pose croisé back.

You must first do a demi-plié on the right leg, and change to a plié on the left leg, with a short movement as if stamping with the left foot. This brings the right foot sur le cou-de-pied forward, and from there continue the step.

Coupé back is done in the same manner.

Coupé can be done in other forms as may be required by the particular movement to be executed. (*See*, grand jeté).

FLIC-FLAC

Flic-flac is done in exercises and in adagio as a connecting link between movements. When first taught in exercise it is linked to some other pas, for instance, battement tendu.

Flic-flac en dehors in beginners' classes is taught in a much simpler version than when it later appears as a linking or passing movement in the finished dance. You begin to learn it in two counts, as follows:

The foot is opened in 2nd position; with a small swing and with pointed toes it glides through 5th position to a little further than sur le cou-de-pied back. This point is reached inevitably because of the "lashing" character of the movement; you then fling the foot back into 2nd position, and with a similar movement swing

45. Flic-flac

*See Supplement, note 10.

the foot in front, where it will again go a little beyond sur le cou-de-pied. Open again into 2nd position.

In more advanced classes flic-flac is done in one count, and with a rise on half-toe on the last movement.

Flic-flac en dedans is done in exactly the same manner, the only difference being that the first passing of the foot is in front, and the second back.

Later it is done en tournant.

FLIC-FLAC EN TOURNANT

En dehors. You begin with the leg and arms open in 2nd position; at the first movement the arms come together below, as if giving the torso the impetus for the turn en dehors. During the second movement, when the foot goes forward, the required pose is taken. The first movement is done en face, the second on a turn. The turn is done on half-toe, and the required pose is held.

En dedans. This is done in reverse. The first movement of the foot is forward and the body turns en dedans. Finish in the required pose.*

PASSÉ

Passé corresponds to its French meaning (passed). It is an auxiliary movement which transfers (passes) the leg from one position into another.

If you are standing in développé effacé forward and you wish to bring the leg back into arabesque without doing a grand rond de jambe, you bend the leg at the knee, leaving it at a height of 90°, brush the toe of that foot past the standing leg and bring it out into arabesque. The passing of the leg through this path is called passé.

The same movement can be done with a jump, leaving the floor with the supporting leg. It will also be called passé.

1   2   1   2

46. Temps relevé

Passé can be done on the floor as in rond de jambe par terre, in which case it will be passé in 1st position.

TEMPS RELEVÉ

The French name for this movement, derived from the French verb *se relever* (to rise) determines its form; relevé is the rising on one leg. This movement is often a preparatory one for another; it assumes a special form when used as a preparation for a turn. This we shall describe later, and now we shall begin with its basic forms: petits and grands relevés.

PETIT RELEVÉ

Stand in 5th position, right foot front. Do a demi-plié, right foot sur le cou-de-pied front; right arm bent in 1st position, left arm out in 2nd position; right leg travels forward and without stopping opens into 2nd position at 45°; simultaneously right arm opens into 2nd position while left foot rises on half-toe.

While doing this movement the thigh should remain motionless, the entire change in position to be done with the lower part of the leg, from the knee down, not letting the upper part of the leg change its position. The lower leg extends only as far as the contracted muscles of the thigh will allow.

Relevé back is done in the same manner, beginning with sur le cou-de-pied back, i.e. do the passing movement back, carrying the leg to 2nd position and keeping the upper part of the leg from changing its position, i.e. doing the movement with the part of the leg from the toe to the knee.

Here the leg acquires a new form of movement which we have not yet discussed. This is the moving of the lower leg back and forth without any lifting movement in the upper part of the leg. This will be the foundation for learning turns, because freedom in the play of the lower leg enables the dancer to work without involving the body in the movement.

GRAND RELEVÉ

The beginning is the same as for petits relevés, except that the right leg is bent very high, the toe at the knee; after the demi-plié the leg is thrown into 2nd position at 90° with the same contraction of the muscles of the upper part of the leg as in petit relevé, and with the same passing movement without a stop in développé forward, the same rise on the half-toe, and the same movement of the arms.

The relevé is used as a preparation for turns when they are not begun from both legs: i.e. not from a preparation in 4th or 5th position, but when standing on one leg, while the other is in the air. When we do a relevé as a preparation for a turn, it is done in a different way; the right leg both passes through the 2nd position, without stopping in the passing movement forward, and goes through sur le cou-de-pied, passing the entire way in one count, i.e. while remaining in plié. On the second count the leg does a turn, touching the cou-de-pied of the left leg.

47. Grand temps relevé

In the execution of turns in 2nd position at 90° from grand relevé, the form of grand relevé does not change. The turn is simply added to it.

VII

JUMPS

JUMPS IN classical ballet are highly diversified. In further study we will see that they are divided into two basic groups.

In the first group are the aerial jumps. For these jumps the dancer must impart a great force to the movement, must stop in the air.

In the second group are the movements which, without a literal jump, cannot be made without tearing oneself away from the ground. These movements, however, are not directed up into the air; they are done close to the ground.

Jumps which are not directed into the air but are parallel to the floor include: pas glissade, pas de basque, and jeté en tournant (in the execution of the first part of this movement).

Aerial jumps are divided into four kinds:

1. Jumps from both feet to both feet which are subdivided into: (*a*) those done directly from 5th position, as changement de pieds, échappé, soubresaut; (*b*) done with a movement of one foot from 5th position to the side, as assemblé, sissonne fermée, sissonne fondue, sissonne tombée, pas de chat, failli, chassé, cabriole fermée, jeté fermé fondu.

2. Jumps from both feet to one foot, which have the following subdivisions: (*a*) when at the beginning the dancer tears himself away from the floor with both feet and finishes the movement on one foot (in a pose), as sissonne ouverte, sissonne soubresaut, ballonné, ballotté, rond de jambe en l'air sauté; (*b*) when the movement begins with a thrusting out of the leg (a take off) and ends with a stop on the same foot in a pose, as jeté from 5th position, grand jeté from 5th position, jeté with a movement in a half-turn, emboité.

3. Jumps from one foot to the other, as jeté entrelacé, saut de basque, jeté passé, jeté in attitude (when it is done from a preparation in 4th position croisé).

4. Combination jumps, the structure of which embodies several elements, as jeté renversé, sissonne renversée, grand pas de basque, double rond de jambe, pas ciseaux, balancé, jeté en tournant and grand fouetté.

Aerial jumps can be small and big, but no matter what their form, the action of leaving the floor must always be clearly visible.

In the development of the jump the following instructions should be followed:

1. Every jump begins with demi-plié. Since the main factor in imparting force at the moment of leaving the floor is the heel, it is necessary, at the development of the jump, to pay special attention to the correctness of demi-plié, i.e. one must see to it that the heels are not lifted from the floor in demi-plié.

2. If the jump is done on both legs, the legs must be forcefully extended in the knees, arches and toes at the moment of the jump. If the jump is done on one leg, the other assumes the position required by the pose. In this case the upper part of the leg must be fully turned out, the back must be straight, the buttocks should not protrude.

3. After the jump the feet must touch the floor first with the toe, then softly with the heel, then lowered into demi-plié. After this the knees should be straightened.

Elevation consists of two elements: elevation proper and ballon.

Elevation in the proper sense of the word is a flight. A man leaves the ground and does a high jump in the air. But such a jump can be meaningless, just an acrobatic feat. A circus acrobat can jump over ten people in a row. His dexterity will amaze us, but we cannot consider that he has elevation. It is a mechanical trick, made possible by well-trained muscles. In dance elevation, ballon must be added to the jump.

Under the term ballon, we understand the ability of a dancer to hold in the air a pose or position, which is customary for him on the ground. The dancer stops in the air, remains there as if suspended. Consequently, when we speak of classic elevation we deal with high jumps connected with ballon.

Elevation is developed through a number of movements. For the development of the jump ending on both feet, we use changement de pieds; for the development of the jump ending on one foot with a movement forward, back and to the side—"the springboard type"—we use pas ballonné. These preparatory steps for high elevation must be done with great perseverance and attention and in great numbers.

The study of jumps is approached gradually. For children and beginners the following serves as the initial exercise:

Stand in 1st position, demi-plié, push off with the heels, and jump, extending the toes and arching the feet. Coming down, touch the floor with the toes and, in the next moment, lower yourself on the heels into demi-plié, and then straighten the knees.

48. Temps levé on two feet

The same thing is done from the 2nd and 5th positions. These jumps are called temps levé. Subsequently, during the study of temps levé in the middle of the floor, it is often done on one foot, i.e. one foot does the jump, the other keeps the position taken before the jump. After this we turn to changement de pieds.

CHANGEMENT DE PIEDS

PETIT CHANGEMENT DE PIEDS

Stand in 5th position, right foot front, demi-plié, push off from the floor, jump up, extending the toes and arching the feet. Coming down, change the feet, left foot will then be front. Come down as in temps levé: first the toes then heels, finishing the movement in demi-plié in 5th position.

49. Petit changement de pieds

This method develops softness and elasticity of the jump, ridding it of its hardness.

70

For more advanced pupils I prefer a different variation of petit changement de pieds. Everything is done as before, but the jump does not tear the feet away from the floor. The toes are touching the floor all the time, as if you were only rising on your toes. The movement is done in an uninterrupted series, without any pause on the plié, although it must be said that the accent is made not into the air, but into the floor, on the plié.

In this manner the exercise is still more energetic and effective in its results.

It is used at the conclusion of exercises in the centre (after allegro) in a fast tempo.

GRAND CHANGEMENT DE PIEDS

For this exercise demi-plié is done deeper and with greater effort in order to rise higher. Push off forcefully from the floor with the heels, bring the legs together and hold them this way until the very last moment and only then change them. Lower yourself in the same way as in petit changement de pieds.

The bigger the jump, the deeper should be the demi-plié before it. Attention must be paid that the heel, due to the strain, should not be lifted from the floor.

Italian   Russian
50. Grand changement de pieds

When changing the legs in the air do not move them far apart. If you do that, you will lose the form of changement de pieds, because this step is a change of feet in the 5th position. The legs should be moved apart only as much as is needed for the transfer, no more.

At the beginning of the study of jumps, attention must be paid to the arms, which must remain absolutely relaxed from the shoulders to the hands, slightly curved, as in the preparatory position; they must not jerk as if trying to help the movement of the legs.

71

In the Italian school it is customary to bend the knees when doing changement de pieds.

PAS ÉCHAPPÉ

PETIT ÉCHAPPÉ

Demi-plié in 5th position, push off with the heels, and immediately, with extended toes and straightened knees, jump into 2nd position in demi-plié, adhering strictly to the directions given for plié in 2nd position. Return with the same kind of a jump, with extended toes and straightened knees, finishing in 5th position.

This pas can also be done in 4th position croisé and effacé, giving the arms an appropriate pose. In general, however, during small jumps the poses of the arms should not be high. The high positions of the arms should be left for big jumps.

In doing échappé one must watch that the plié on both feet is even; special attention to this must be paid when doing échappé in 4th position.

51. Petit échappé

Échappé can be done with a finish on one foot. The entire pas is the same as above, only the finish is different. The feet do not return into 5th position, but one of them goes sur le cou-de-pied front or back. This échappé is done in 4th position as well as 2nd.

GRAND ÉCHAPPÉ

In petit échappé, in the jump, the legs open immediately in 2nd position. In grand échappé extend the legs, after a deep demi-plié, in a closed 5th position during the highest possible jump, and only coming down, open them into 2nd position. Return to 5th position also from a high jump, forcefully pushing off from the floor with the heels.

52. Grand échappé

This échappé can also be finished on one foot, coming down into an attitude, arabesque, or développé forward at 90°, i.e. generally into a big pose.

PAS ASSEMBLÉ

Assemblé is the basis for the development of the jump in general. For beginners it is the solid foundation of the dance and the first step toward it.

In spite of the fact that assemblé is fairly complicated, it is one of the first steps to be taught to beginners. It is brought into classroom exercises early, because if the pupils understand assemblé further study will be easier for them.

I   2   3   4

53. Assemblé

Stand in 5th position, right foot front; demi-plié, with a sliding movement draw left leg to the side, and with the toe of the extended foot reach 2nd position on the floor; with right foot, which has remained in plié, push off the floor, extending the toes; then, both feet simultaneously, return to 5th position in demi-plié left foot front. From this plié the movement is repeated with the other leg, thus the execution of this pas constitutes a small progression forward.

One must pay attention to the exactness of 2nd position, i.e. not let the foot deviate into écarté forward or back; exactness during the elementary study of this step insures the subsequent correct execution of its more complex form, the large assemblé.

Assemblé is also done backwards in the following manner: from 5th position, the front foot is drawn out into 2nd position, and at the finish placed into 5th position back.

In this manner (in two counts) assemblé is taught at the beginning.

In the next, more complicated form, the leg passes 2nd position at the height of 45° with a passing movement, without an accent in the 2nd position. This assemblé is done in one count. After this form we turn to the large assemblé.

In the large assemblé, done backwards, right leg is thrust out to 90°, as in grand battement; the subsequent jump—a big one— carries the dancer to the side. At this moment the left leg must be in front of the right one and the legs held closed in the air, then the dancer lowers himself, on both legs simultaneously, into 5th position in demi-plié.

In order to create an impression of a higher jump, the Italians bend their knees after grand battement, before lowering themselves into 5th position. This bending of the knees during the jump renders the dance a grotesque character, spoiling its classic line.

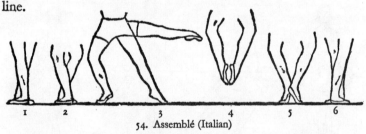

| 1 | 2 | 3 | 4 | 5 | 6 |

54. Assemblé (Italian)

The large assemblé is usually done during the most winning moment of the execution of a dance. In order to have enough force for such a large movement, it is most effective to do just before it an auxiliary movement either in the form of a glissade or in the form of the following preparation: do a grand développé forward, fall on that foot in plié and push off forcefully, thrusting the other leg into 2nd position at 90°; the push-off then is more energetic and the entire movement gains in its effect.

In general, to make a jump stand out and to heighten its effect, it should be preceded and followed, not by a movement of equal size and strength, but by a smaller movement. One of the movements gains in its effect from the other.

I don't bring participation of the arms into the elementary study of assemblé, but strive to achieve in the pupils a free position of the arms, without stiffness and jerking.

When the pupils have mastered assemblé, one may introduce into it arm movements. The hands open at the same time as the leg goes into 2nd position, and they close in the final 5th position, joining into the preparatory position. Later on, the head begins to take part in the movement. At the movement of the leg and the arms into 2nd position, the head must be held in profile to the side opposite the leg which is being opened, and at the conclusion of assemblé, the head is turned to the opposite side, also in profile. I indicate that the head must be turned in profile, because an indefinite turn of the head makes it look as if one were bending to the shoulder, and this creates a soft, weak impression.

In the advanced classes, when assemblé is done in its simple form and slow tempo, I do not require participation of the arms. Only in the more complicated combinations, which are designed for dancers and not students, do I include arm movements in assemblé. Assemblé can be done in all directions, forward, back, croisé, effacé, etc.

In class one must demand a precise finish of assemblé in 5th position. It happens that on the stage, during the actual dance, one is forced, once in a while, to execute a step not as precisely as it should be. To guard against loss of precision, the dancer, through daily exercises done assiduously and pedantically, must preserve and uphold the developed forms of the dance. The more a dancer practices in the classroom, the fewer mistakes will he make on the stage. This is the object of the daily classroom exercises.

PAS JETÉ

The French name of this step is very expressive; the French verb *jeter* means to throw, and the term jeté depicts the throwing of the leg and the falling onto it. But the step jeté acquires this character only in its finished form, grand jeté. For the beginning the following exercise is used.

Stand in 5th position, right foot front; demi-plié, left leg is drawn to the side in a gliding movement, the knee and toes are straightened and the toes touch the floor in 2nd position. Then push off the floor with the right foot in a jump, straightening the knee and toes, return the left leg to the place formerly held

55. Pas jeté

by the right leg and lower yourself on it in demi-plié. Bring the right foot sur le cou-de-pied back.

This is the movement forward. In the movement backwards, the leg which is in front goes to the side. The position sur le cou-de-pied is also in front.

Further, jeté can be done in all directions, gradually developing the style of the dance, doing it with arms in various small poses, and then progressing to the study of jeté with the leg at 45° and to the grand jeté with the leg at 90°, and big poses.

It is proper to mention here the difference in the approach to jeté in the Italian school. The Italian school teaches the pupil to throw up the legs very high and to bend them sharply; the movement acquires a great strain and the design acquires a definitely grotesque shade.

GRAND JETÉ

For execution on the stage, grand jeté demands an entirely different approach from the small jeté.

It is done not from 5th position, but is preceded by a preliminary movement of a spring-board nature. This is the necessary

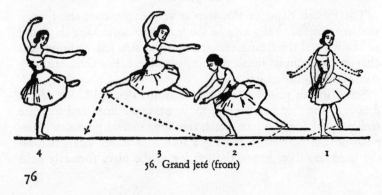

56. Grand jeté (front)

transitory movement before every big jump and leap. It is necessary to send the body forward, it is necessary to push off from something.

There are various methods for doing that: one can do pas couru, glissade, or coupé, whichever gives the necessary push-off. Men very often substitute a wide careless run. I prefer a more complicated approach which brings into work the entire body and the arms. From this approach the concluding pose emanates as a logical result. It is coupé of the following kind:

Stand in pose croisé, right foot back. Forcefully transferring weight of the body to the right leg, move the leg forward to 4th position effacé with a strong push to the floor and squat on it, bending the entire body to this leg, push off the floor, throw up the left leg to 90° forward and jump onto it, trying to remain in the air in a definitely expressed attitude or arabesque.

The arms will move the following way: when the body is forcefully bent to the right, the arms will be thrown up into 2nd position; when the entire weight is transferred on to the right leg, the arms come together in the preparatory pose below, they should, as it were, lend force for the leap. The required pose is reached by the arms moving through 1st position.

There exists, although it is seldom used, a grand jeté back which is done in the following manner: start; left foot front croisé, shift the body forcefully onto the left foot back in effacé plié and, pushing off from it, thrust right leg back croisé to 90° and jump onto it, assuming the pose développé forward. The movement of the arms is the same as in grand jeté forward.

57. Grand jeté (back)

JETÉ FERMÉ

Stand in 5th position, right foot front; demi-plié, throw up left leg to the side as high as possible, jump onto it, transferring the weight of the entire body on to this leg. The right leg opens to the side at the same height as the left one. Lower yourself in plié and close the right leg front in 5th position.

58. Jeté fermé

This movement is done in two counts; plié on the pick-up, first count—transfer of weight on the left leg in plié after the fall on it, second count—the final 5th position.

At the initial plié in 5th position the arms are in preparatory position, from the moment when the leg is thrust out to the side and until the final 5th position, the movement of the arms goes simultaneously with the movement of the legs, i.e. they too open to 2nd position. The head also moves from right to left.

There exists also a different ending for jeté fermé: at the end the leg is put down softly and gradually. In this case, the movement is called jeté fondu (melting).

This jeté is done forward, back, in effacé, croisé, and écarté. The arms follow the ordered pose.

JETÉ WITH A MOVEMENT TO THE SIDE IN HALF-TURNS

Stand in 5th position, right foot front, demi-plié; take right leg to the side to the 2nd position for jeté (right arm in 1st position, left—in 2nd), change to that foot in a jump moving to the right side as far as possible in a half-turn. Stop in demi-plié with the back to the audience, left foot sur le cou-de-pied back, left arm in 1st position, right—in 2nd.

The head is turned in profile to the left shoulder. Continuing the movement, take left leg to the side to the 2nd position, remaining with the back to the audience, fly to the left in a jump, and only at the last moment do a half-turn in the air. Stop in demi-plié, right foot sur le cou-de-pied front. The left arm accompanies the movement of the left leg, i.e. it opens in 2nd position, the right one bends at the conclusion to 1st position, the head is turned en face.

In this manner the first turn is en dedans, the second—en dehors.

This jeté can also be done to the other side. Stand in 5th position, left foot front, begin the movement with the right, turning en dehors, finishing with the left foot sur le cou-de-pied front, and stopping in demi-plié with the back to the audience, left arm in 1st position, right one in 2nd, the head—in profile toward the left shoulder. Then continue the movement to the left with a turn en dedans and finishing with the right foot sur le cou-de-pied back.

| 5 | 4 | 3 | 2 | 1 |
| two | | one | | up beat |

59. Jeté with progression toward a half-turn

The right arm is in 1st position, the left one in 2nd, the head—en face.

In the first case it is necessary to leave the body en face until the turn, and in the second case to leave it with the back to the audience.

The head should be turned in profile.

JETÉ PASSÉ

Stand in pose croisé, right foot behind. Change onto right

| 1 | 2 | 3 | 4 |

60. Jeté passé (front)

foot in 4th position, effacé forward, demi-plié, taking body forward, extend arm straight forward, keeping both shoulders level; i.e. not inclining right shoulder toward right leg. During the demi-plié throw left leg back and high. With a jump put left foot in the place of the right one, throw right leg into attitude croisée, bend the back backward.

Jeté passé back is done in the same manner, i.e. stand at the beginning croisé, left foot front, change onto the left foot in 4th position effacé back, in demi-plié, bend body to that leg; both arms open into 2nd position with open palms, keeping the shoulders level. Squat on left foot, thrust right one high forward and with a jump place it on the spot of the left one, then, throwing the left leg to 90°, forward in croisé, assume required pose, i.e. the body and the head may be turned right or left corresponding to the turn of the body.

1   2   3   4
61. Jeté passé (back)

JETÉ RENVERSÉ

From demi-plié in 5th position throw the leg with a grand battement into 2nd position at 90°, open arms in 2nd position, palms down; jump onto the raised foot into attitude croisée stopping in it in plié and do renversé en dehors, finishing it in 5th position.

1   2   3   4   5   6
62. Jeté renversé en dehors

The same movement can be done backward, i.e. after one of the legs is thrown into 2nd position, bring the other one, after the jump, forward at 90° in croisé and do renversé en dedans.

See to it that the jump is finished croisé and that renversé is done correctly, i.e. that this is not done with the back to the audience. This will happen if the back is turned too soon while jumping in attitude, or in the reverse pose développé forward, mentioned above.

63. Jeté renversé en dedans

In this movement one should not rise on half-toe after the jeté, but one should join it to the following renversé, through pas de bourrée, i.e. step on the other foot on half-toe and conclude renversé.

JETÉ ENTRELACÉ

We begin to study this step moving from the right front corner of the classroom diagonally to left back corner, so as to face the audience all the time. This way it is easier to understand the step. Later on the step can be done moving from the back diagonally to the front. In this case all stops will be with the back to the audience.

Stand in pose effacé back, right foot forward, demi-plié, left

81

leg is raised to 45°, body bends forward, left arm is forward, as in the 2nd arabesque. Open arms into 2nd position, change into demi-plié on the left leg; with a wide step diagonally back push off the left foot, thrusting the right leg to 90° forward to point 6 and, joining the arms in 1st position, jump on to the right leg, turning to the left. During the jumps the legs appear to inter-lace (this is the reason for calling this movement entrelacé, i.e. interlaced), only at this moment turn the body a full turn, throwing up the arms; i.e. hold the body en face, so that the turn takes place during the jump. Finish in arabesque or in attitude.

64. Jeté entrelacé

When you throw over the right leg, take care that it passes through 1st position. This will help to preserve the interlacing of the legs; also try to come down after the jump on the same spot, otherwise the legs pass too widely open, and the movement loses its correct design. To prevent the body from dragging and to make it help the movement, the arms should gain their force in 2nd position during the change to the left foot. In this lies their help to the entire movement.

JETÉ EN TOURNANT PAR TERRE

This jeté is called par terre because its direction is not into the air but horizontal.

As an example, let us take jeté en tournant par terre which progresses diagonally from the left back corner of the classroom to its right front corner.

Stand in 5th position, right foot front, demi-plié; diagonally in the direction of effacé throw out right foot with a gliding move-ment on the floor, fall on it in plié, pushing off with the left foot. The right arm in the same direction, the left one—to the side in the 2nd position.

The left foot leaves the floor not more than at 45° and the entire figure acquires a long stretched-out form, the type of an

82

5   4   3   2   1

65. Jeté en tournant (par terre)

arabesque. Pull the left leg to the right one—with a light jump, joining the feet in 5th position, making a full turn to the right. Land on the left leg in demi-plié, right foot sur le cou-de-pied, front.

Usually this jeté is done a consecutive number of times.

JETÉ EN TOURNANT

Begin with the preparatory movement. Stand in 5th position, right foot front. Do a small sissonne tombée forward with the right foot to 4th position croisé into a demi-plié on the right foot; then bring the left foot close to the 5th back and transfer the weight of the body on to it in demi-plié. The right leg is thrown out forward at 90°, and it describes a circle in the air while the body is turned to the right. In turning, jump onto the right foot and fall into attitude croisée, not letting yourself be carried away by the momentum, and at the same time, not bending much to the right at the concluding attitude.

1   2   3   4

66. Jeté en tournant

In order to acquire force in the sissonne tombée, bend the body forward forcefully; in changing to the left foot, bend the body effacé and incline the head in the same direction, and from here describe an arc with the body.

During the preparatory sissonne tombée the right arm is bent in 1st position in front of the body, the left arm is open in 2nd position. When the weight of the body is transferred to the left leg in demi-plié, the arms join in 1st position to gain force. The arms finish in attitude.*

SISSONNE

There are many different forms of sissonne. Let us analyse the following most commonly used.

SISSONNE SIMPLE

The elementary study of sissonne begins with its simplest form. 5th position, demi-plié, jump, during which the legs are joined, knees and toes extended, as in every jump. After the jump, lower yourself on one foot in demi-plié, the other foot sur le cou-de-pied, and finish with assemblé.

SISSONNE OUVERTE (OPEN)

Sissonne ouverte is a development of the foregoing movement, i.e. after the jump up, the leg, being carried through sur le cou-de-pied, opens in a pose at 45° to the side in the 2nd position, to the forward, or back.

67. Sissonne ouverte en écarté at 90°

In order to gain balance, beginners may lower the leg after the jump and open it into 2nd position, front, or back with the toe on the floor.

The arms take the position corresponding to the ordered pose. In the advanced classes the jump is higher and stronger, and the leg is lifted to 90° in attitude, arabesque, écarté forward and back, etc. In perfecting sissonne ouverte you may do it flying to the

*See Supplement, note 12.

side. If you do it forward, the pose will be attitude or arabesque back. When the jump is backwards, the raised leg will take the pose forward. For écarté, jump to the side, etc., depending on the direction of the required pose.

In the intermediate and advanced classes a more complicated form of sissonne ouverte en tournant is used. It is executed in the following manner: after demi-plié the right arm goes into 1st position, the left one into 2nd, and in this way force is taken for the turn in the air. One should pay attention that the right shoulder does not go forward before the jump. Push off with the heels, rise in the air, and doing a turn in the air, open the leg during the turn. Finish by stopping in the ordered pose at 45° or 90°.

SISSONNE FERMÉE (CLOSED)

As an example I shall analyse here one form of sissonne fermée; all others are done the same way, all that changes is the direction.

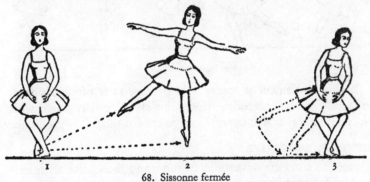

68. Sissonne fermée

Sissonne Fermée, Écarté en Avant. 5th position, right foot front, demi-plié, the jump is not up but to the side; the entire body flies to left; right leg opens into 2nd position, and when the left foot steps on the floor, the right one closes in 5th position together with the left one; the right foot is brought to the left one with the toe gliding on the floor. The jump is not big, and the leg is not raised high.

SISSONNE FONDUE

If we want to do a high jump with the leg raised to 90°, we get not a sissonne fermée, but a sissonne fondue. A high développé will not allow the right leg to finish the jump simultaneously with the left one, and the joining of the legs will assume the character of fondue; the toe should not glide over the floor, but the foot should be softly put on the floor, slightly bending the leg. The arms and head work are in correspondence with the required pose. In this manner sissonne fondue is studied in the advanced classes.

SISSONNE TOMBÉE

5th position, right foot front, demi-plié, jump with both feet in the air. With a passing movement the right foot is placed sur le cou-de-pied or at the knee, depending on whether the step is to be big or small. Fall in plié on left leg, the right leg is immediately taken out in the required direction croisé or effacé, then fall on it in plié as if belatedly.

69. Sissonne tombée

If this movement precedes a big jump, as it often happens, especially in the masculine dance, this sissonne may finish with pas de bourrée, which is very convenient for the following jump.

SISSONNE RENVERSÉE

First do sissonne ouverte in attitude, and then finish with renversé. One should not rise on half-toe after the jump in attitude, but the jump should be joined with the next movement, renversé, through pas de bourrée, i..e step on the other foot on half-toe and conclude renversé.

SISSONNE SOUBRESAUT

Sissonne soubresaut is executed as sissonne ouverte, but at the beginning of the jump from the 5th position both heels are held together, as in soubresaut. At the beginning of the jump the body bends forward and during the flight forcefully bends back. The execution must be very precise, the legs, during the flight, should not open and beat each other, so as to avoid getting a form of a cabriole from 5th position. It is effective and convenient to execute this pas several consecutive times, diagonally in attitude effacée,

86

adding, after the fall in plié, in attitude on the right leg, a coupé with the left leg, and assemblé with the right forward, moving in the direction of écarté (point 2).

70. Sissonne soubresaut

SOUBRESAUT

Soubresaut is a jump from both feet onto both feet.

Push off the floor, fly forward with extended arches and toes without opening the legs and feet. Before the beginning of the jump the body inclines forward at the beginning and then forcefully bends back, so that the legs remain at the back. Attention should be paid that in joining the legs the calves do not hit each other, otherwise you get a form of cabriole. Many make this mistake.

71. Soubresaut

To get the correct form, the legs should not be joined in their full length; join forcefully the lower parts of the soles.

Lower yourself simultaneously on both feet. The arms in soubresaut are free and depend only on the general design of the dance.

87

ROND DE JAMBE EN L'AIR SAUTÉ

The study of rond de jambe en l'air sauté begins in the following manner: after doing sissonne ouverte to the side in 2nd position, do rond de jambe en l'air with a simultaneous jump on the supporting foot. Double rond de jambe is done in the same manner. In subsequent studies rond de jambe en l'air is done with a simultaneous jump from demi-plié in 5th position. At the beginning this movement is done with the leg raised to 45°, and later, in the advanced classes, with the leg raised to 90°.

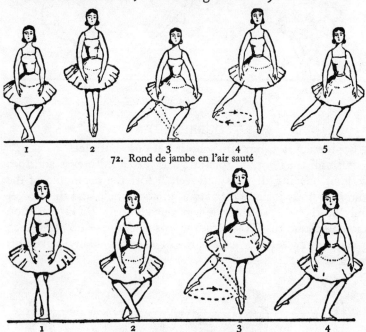

72. Rond de jambe en l'air sauté

73. Rond de jambe en l'air sauté

PAS DE CHAT

Stand in 5th position, left foot front. Throw the right leg, half-bent, back into 45° croisé, at the same time do demi-plié on the left foot. Push off with the left foot, throwing the left leg, half-bent, back in effacé to meet the right one. There must be a moment when both feet are in the air at the same time, passing each other. Keeping the upper part of the legs turned out, and without opening them too wide, fall first on the right foot, then on the left one. The left foot passes forward into 4th position. One may finish it also in 5th position.

When the body is on the left foot it should have a slight tilt forward, to give it a chance to bend more backward.

At the moment when both feet are in the air, the entire body bends backward, the waist forcefully arched. This pas is embellished by the position of the head. The head may be held in various ways, as long as it correctly follows the movement.

74. Pas de chat

The arms fly up with a soft movement: the right one in 2nd position, the left one forward from the preparatory position into a not-too-high level. The hands are dropped at the beginning, but later are thrown upward. The character of the movement of the arms is analogous to the character of the movement of the legs; the same soft throws which explains the name of the movement—cat-like.

The Italian pas de chat lacks this cat-like character. If the left leg is thrown to the side softly, the right one, which began the movement, is thrown into 2nd position in a dry manner, and the body, usually, does not underline the softness of the entire *pas*.

PAS DE BASQUE

This movement is in three counts and is done the following way:

Stand in 5th position, right foot front. On the up-beat (*and*): demi-plié, slightly throwing up the arms towards 2nd position before the beginning of the movement; right foot glides forward, croisé, and describes a half-circle, en dehors (the left foot remains in plié).

On *one*, jump onto the right foot in demi-plié without getting off the floor; (the arms at this moment join in the preparatory position). On *two*—the left foot, opened in 2nd position with toes extended, glides through 1st position into croisé forward. On *three*, the final count, a jump is made which joins both feet in 5th

89

position in demi-plié. This jump is done close to the floor. With a gliding movement both feet move forward with extended toes, without leaving the floor, and end in 5th position. This manner of execution justifies the importance of the movement as a jump par terre. On *two* the arms move through 1st position, and on *three* the hands open slightly. From here the movement continues, the arms moving through 2nd position, etc.

75. Pas de basque

Pas de basque backward is done the same way.

5th position, right foot front, demi-plié, left foot glides back, describing a half-circle en dedans, jump on left foot; right foot glides through 1st position backward in croisé demi-plié, and on *three*—the feet join with the same gliding jump, only backward. The arms move the same way.

GRAND PAS DE BASQUE

To lend the jump more force, this pas is done with arms thrown up. At the beginning throw the arms into 2nd position, and carrying them through the preparatory and 1st positions, lift them into 3rd. The feet do all movements in big positions. The right foot describes a big half-circle en dehors at 90°, the left leg in demi-plié; carrying the right foot to 2nd position, do a big jump onto the right foot (arms in 3rd position), the left leg is bent and thrown out forward at 90°, the arms are gradually opened into 2nd position. The left foot is lowered to the floor forward in croisé, and both feet are pulled into the final pose, as in the small pas de basque. To give this pas a final polish, bend the head and body forward at the beginning of the movement, and lift them at the moment when the arms are thrown out into 3rd position.

To do the movement backward, describe a circle with the left foot en dedans, carrying the leg into 2nd position at 90°, jump on left foot, right foot is bent high and moves, opening backward.

76. Grand pas de basque

Fall on right foot back in croisé. The end of the movement and the arms are the same as in the pas forward.

SAUT DE BASQUE

Stand in 5th position, right foot front. Do a coupé with right foot without a jump, lifting it to the knee, and simultaneously press left heel to the floor in demi-plié. Move right foot, extending it into 2nd position with a passing movement, following that make a half turn on it to the right, thrusting left leg into 2nd position at 90°, towards point 2. Complete the turn with a jump, travelling to the side in the direction of thrust-out left leg, so as not to remain on the same spot during the jump, fall on left foot in demi-plié, while right leg bends to the knee. This bending is done right after the foot leaves the floor and without any additional movements with the leg, as is often observed when the step is executed incorrectly. Both legs in this pas should be fully turned out, especially the right one as its knee is forcefully turned to the side.

77. Saut de basque

The arms move the following way: at the beginning right arm is bent in 1st position, left one—in 2nd; during the transfer of the body to right leg, right arm goes into 2nd position simultaneously with left leg, left arm moves with a strong thrust below through 1st position, which gives strength to the jump. At the instant of the jump, left arm is bent in 1st position, right one extended into 2nd. At the return to left leg, the arms also return to the initial position.

The arms may also be thrust upward into 3rd position; in this case they are thrust to the side from the initial position half-way up, through the preparatory and 1st positions, and are lifted all the way up during the jump, so as to give oneself a good lift.

In this manner, as the jump is repeated several times, the arms do not return to the initial position but are extended to the side, and from there, through the preparatory position, they are swung for the succeeding jump.*

GARGOUILLADE

This old French term has remained in the Italian school. In the Russian school we call this step rond de jambe double.

Stand in 5th position, right foot front. At the initial demi-plié right leg does rond de jambe en l'air en dehors; when this movement is finished and the leg is open in 2nd position, transfer with a jump to right leg in demi-plié. Simultaneously left leg does rond de jambe en l'air en dehors, but begins and ends it at the calf of right leg; after this left leg moves forward on the floor into croisé in demi-plié.

As this movement is usually a passing one, the arm movement is governed by the preceding and succeeding poses.

This step en dedans is seldom done on the stage, but is used in class. It is done in the following manner: stand in 5th position, right foot front, begin with left leg rond de jambe en l'air

*See Supplement, note 13.

78. Gargouillade (rond de jambe double)

en dedans and, transferring on to it with a jump in demi-plié, do rond de jambe en dedans beginning and ending it at the calf and move the leg backwards, following the instructions given for en dehors.

PAS DE CISEAUX

Stand in croisé back, right foot back; plié on left leg, and with a short and strong grand battement, thrust right leg forward in effacé to 90°, throwing the body back. Left leg joins right one in the air, and immediately, extended, moves back on the floor through 1st position into 1st arabesque, while right one is lowered to the floor in plié. The characteristic moment here is when both legs are in the air. This change of legs is done in one count.

This form of pas de ciseaux is used for study; for the stage

1   2   3   4

79. Pas de ciseaux

dance there exists another approach which is more effective. When, after the execution of a given step, you stop in a pose with left leg in croisé forward lifted to 90°, you should do a coupé on it, thrusting right leg, etc. The body is fully involved in this movement. It is forcefully bent back during the passing of one leg by the other in the air, and is later thrust forward into arabesque.

The arms are held at the beginning in front in 1st position, and then they take the pose of arabesque.

PAS BALLOTTÉ

This is a very difficult movement to execute in its correct form. It requires strength in the legs and body and girls seldom succeed in it. Usually, they simplify it very much and bring it down to jumping up and thrusting the leg forward and back, bending it so much, in addition, that ballotté loses entirely its original form.

80. Pas ballotté: 3, 2, 1—front; 1, 2, 3—back

The term ballotté is very picturesque; it evokes the vision of a boat rocking on waves, and a well-executed ballotté does resemble such rocking. No stop, no pause, is noticed in the movement. The dancer swings in the air, with her legs closed and extended, forward and back, passing a point which lies in the centre of this movement. The body is forcefully bent back and then thrust forward, which, when the legs are extended, forms a specific design reminiscent of nonchalant rocking.

Ballotté is done in the following manner:

Stand in croisé back, right foot forward. Demi-plié on right foot, join the legs in a jump in 5th position, moving them in the air past the point on which you were originally standing and, bending the body back (which helps the movement a great deal) fall on the left foot in demi-plié, open the right one in effacé, and without bending it, push off, again joining the legs in 5th position, move them past the point on which you were originally standing and bend the body forward. Fall on the right foot in demi-plié, left leg in effacé back at the necessary height.

The legs should be as much extended as possible, the body and the legs should form one unit. Then we succeed in getting the soft, wave-like rocking. The arms are balanced with the legs. At the stop in the forward movement, the left arm is bent into 1st

94

position, the right one extended to the side in 2nd position; at the stop on the right foot, the right arm is in 1st position, the left one in 2nd position. The change of arms is done softly, and they pass their original positions.

It is more convenient to begin to study ballotté from 5th position; do demi-plié, joining the legs into 5th position during the jump, press the soles firmly together, with the toes extended, at the beginning of the jump, and in this manner fly forward from the spot on which you were standing at the beginning, fall on left foot in demi-plié, right leg open in effacé forward at 45°.

Conclude by doing assemblé. In the same manner ballotté is also done backwards, i.e. after the jump from 5th position fly back with both feet from the spot you were standing at the beginning, fall on right foot in plié in effacé at 45° and conclude with assemblé.

PAS BALLONNÉ

Stand in 5th position, right foot front, demi-plié; gliding the right foot into 2nd position at 45°, push off the floor with the left foot, toes extended, and fly over, as it were, towards the toe of the right foot, lowering yourself on the left foot in demi-plié, at the same time bending the right one sur le cou-de-pied.

Often, when teaching children, teachers do not pay attention to the correct placing of the foot sur le cou-de-pied. The foot is carried past the other leg, the legs cross, and the resulting pose is both incorrect and bad looking.

Ballonné is done in all directions: effacé, croisé forward and

4   3   2   1

81. Pas ballonné effacé (front)

back, écarté forward and back. The arms should be placed according to the direction of the movement. For instance, when you do ballonné en effacé with the right foot, the left arm may be bent in 1st position and the right one extended to the side. But if you change the body the least bit, turning the right shoulder forward, you get a jump in écarté. In this case it is better to bend the right arm and to extend the left one, bending the body slightly back and left, as it is required by the pose. One may also lift one or both arms up, in 3rd position.

In grand ballonné (at 90°), the foot may be bent to the knee, but in the small ballonné, the form is more correct if the foot is placed sur le cou-de-pied.

In the execution of ballonné, the body and the arms must not move during the jump, but remain in the pose, so that one should notice no strain or jerking.*

PAS CHASSÉ

This pas is seldom used in the feminine dance, but more often in the masculine. Usually it is done several times in succession.

Stand in 5th position, right foot front, demi-plié, jump up, right leg opens into 2nd position at 45° (sissonne tombée to the right), but with a more passing movement than usual, the left

| 6 | 5 | 4 | | 3 | 2 | 1 |

82. Pas chassé

leg is drawn in a gliding movement to the right one, the legs join during the jump in the air, very straight, in 5th position, with the toes extended and touching. At this moment the jump must be as high as possible. Immediately, the right leg opens again, and the movement continues.

Pas chassé is done to all sides in required poses.

GLISSADE

It would seem that the very name of this step indicates the gliding characteristic of it. Yet we see that this movement is very seldom distinguished from other movements, and is lost on the stage. In the male dance especially it is difficult to see what is a glissade and what is just a simple running start for a leap.

96   *See Supplement, note 14.

This is bad for the dancer, because a properly executed glissade helps the leap, while a running start, with the legs thrown to this side and the other, tends to offset the whole body from the proper manner of doing the leap, and the leap loses its beauty and force.

Glissade may be done with or without a change of feet. At the beginning glissade is practised without change of feet. It is this form of the glissade that I shall analyse here.

Stand in 5th position, right foot front. Demi-plié, right foot with toe pointed glides along the floor to 2nd position and reaches it with the extended toe; immediately after that the body travels towards and onto the right leg without lifting the feet off the floor, then the left foot glides along the floor into 5th position back. Then demi-plié.

This is the basic characteristic of glissade: it begins and it ends with plié. The final plié is the one that helps the following leap,

83. Pas glissade

and for this reason glissade is the best preparation for leaps.

Glissade may be done in different directions and in different poses. It is wrong to do glissade like jeté fermé, but it is also wrong to do it like creeping, without tearing oneself away from the floor.

If you do glissade as a preparatory movement to a big leap, open your arms to the sides at the same time as you open your legs to 2nd position, then close them again to the preparatory position. This will give force to the following leap.

PAS FAILLI

This movement is done on one count, all its changes are run together, and there is a certain characteristic fleeting air about it.

Stand in 5th position, right foot front. Demi-plié, jump up vertically, feet close together. During the jump turn body effacé back; lower yourself into demi-plié on right foot, open left one to 45° in effacé back, and immediately without a pause, move the extended toe of the left foot on the floor through the 1st position forward into croisé, and then—demi-plié.

The proper character of failli can be achieved only with the correct accompaniment of the arms. There should be no underscored movement, the arms should move softly, as if spontaneously. At the beginning of the movement, the arms should be slightly thrown up, then the left arm moves forward together with the left leg, and at the same time the body inclines to the left.

84. Pas failli

One may finish it also differently, moving the arms into a pose, preparation à la pirouette, so that the final pose of failli could serve as a preparation from the 4th position for turns or for some other movement.

PAS EMBOÎTÉ

Stand in 5th position, right foot front. Demi-plié, jump up, right leg bent to 45°; fall on right foot in demi-plié, while in the air move the left leg forward, bending it, jump up again, move the right leg forward. Finish on left foot in demi-plié, the right leg forward and bent.

To do this movement correctly, the bent leg should move beyond the straight one during each change. Emboîté back is done the same way.

Emboîté can also be done high (grand emboîté), that is, at the level of the knee. The leg is thrown out higher and is bent less. On the stage it is very effective to do emboîté in a series, beginning low with a very small one, and gradually throwing the leg up higher and higher, to a grand emboité.

EMBOÎTÉ EN TOURNANT

Stand in 5th position, right foot front. Demi-plié, jump to the side, flying to the right with the entire body and legs, simul-

98

taneously, while in the air move the left leg forward and bend it; lower yourself on right foot in demi-plié with the back to the audience, bending left leg in front of you to 45°, turn in the air with a jump, flying in the same direction and landing on left foot in demi-plié en face, bending right leg in front, and continue the same way.

85. Pas emboîté en tournant

The arms should assist. At the beginning, the right arm is in 1st position, left one open in 2nd. Push off the floor, and during the jump throw the arms to the sides and during the stop with the back to the audience, move the left arm to the 1st position simultaneously with the left leg; at the next turn and jump, throw left arm to the side, and move right one forward together with right foot, etc.

PAS BALANCÉ

This is one of the simple pas allegro which is easily done even by children. In classical dancing it is often used in waltz tempo.

Stand in 5th position, right foot front. From demi-plié do a light jeté with the right foot to the side, and then draw left foot back (on count *one*). On count *two* change to the left foot on half

| 5 | 4 | 3 | 2 | 1 |
| three | two | one | | up beat |

86. Pas balancé

99

toe, and on *three* lower yourself again on right foot in demi-plié, and raise the left one sur le cou-de-pied back.

The next balancé will be to the left, i.e. jeté left, etc.

CABRIOLE

Cabriole is done forward and backward, croisé, effacé, écarté, in arabesque, from 5th position, or from some preparatory pas such as a small sissonne tombée or coupé. The form of the cabriole itself does not change with the direction or preparatory pas, and therefore I shall describe here the most widely used: cabriole in effacé forward.

We begin to practice cabrioles fairly low, and all the following rules for cabriole at 90° apply also to the study of it at 45°.

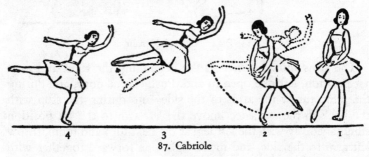

4   3   2   1

87. Cabriole

As in all our examples we do a cabriole from the right foot. To do a cabriole from the right foot, begin with preparation croisé, left foot front; from demi-plié on the left foot, the right leg is thrust up to 90° in effacé forward, the left leg is drawn to the right one and hits it with the calf. The legs must be fully extended, the knees well straightened, toes forcefully pointed. The right leg must not be lowered to meet the hitting left one. Fall on the left foot in demi-plié, keeping the right leg in the pose that was ordered, in this example effacé forward.

Cabriole fermée differs from the described one in that the leg does not remain open, but closes in 5th position. The right leg must finish the movement in the same tempo as the left one, in demi-plié in 5th position.

If cabriole is done forward, the body bends back. Cabriole in the 3rd and 4th arabesques is comfortably done from the same preparation, but the body should be bent more forward—a position which is customary for these arabesques. If cabriole is done in 2nd position or in écarté with the right leg, the preparation should be croisé back with the left leg; at the concluding movement in plié, the body should be forcefully bent to the left. This must be done carefully so as to preserve the correct and beautiful pose. The arms, in all cases, assume the position required by the pose.

For cabrioles in 1st and 2nd arabesques the preparation should be taken from a small sissonne tombée in the direction of the movement.

Cabriole is one of the most difficult forms of the jump. At the beginning of its study one may use the following approach: open right leg in effacé, front at 45°, plié on left foot, and with a jump throw left leg to the right one, hitting the calf, lower yourself on left foot in demi-plié. Cabriole back is done the same way.

In the male dance, cabriole is done double, i.e. the calves of the legs hit each other twice. Very strong dancers may hit even more times. Attention must be paid, however, that the legs open well each time, otherwise the brilliant virtuosity this difficult pas presupposes will be lost.

In general, the study of high cabriole should begin after the difficulties of the other jumps have been overcome. Cabriole is the most difficult and the most complicated jump, requiring a well-developed elevation and ballon.

VIII

BEATS

BEATS, THE general French term for which is *batterie*, are steps in which one leg is beaten against the other. Beats bring into ballet the element of brilliance, virtuosity, and therefore the execution of them does not allow any carelessness, approximation or simplification, or they would lose their raison d'être. In the practice of beats one must adhere to the following rules necessary for a sharp and brilliant beat. During the beat both legs must be equally well extended, one should never beat with one leg while the other is in a passive state. Before each beat one must not forget to open the legs slightly, so as to get a sharp and clear-cut beat. In this manner, when a beat is done from the 5th position at the beginning of the jump, the legs must be slightly opened to the sides. If you don't follow this rule, you'll get a fuzzy smear which will look more like an obstruction to the dance than a virtuoso pas.

If a beat is done with legs opened in advance, i.e. not from 5th position, the legs must again slightly open after the beat and only then assume the required terminating pose.

Beats should not be simplified but, on the contrary, practised in their most complex form. For instance, small beats like royal, entrechat-trois, -quatre, -cinq, should be done close to the floor; this will force you to cross the legs very quickly with a short, sharp movement. This is much more difficult, but there is more compactness, energy, and brilliance in such beats. If these small beats are done during a big jump, high in the air, you have enough time to do the beats, but the performance loses in brilliance.

There are three classifications of beats: pas battus, entrechats, and brisés.

PAS BATTUS

Any step embellished with a beat is called pas battu. When the pupils begin to do the more difficult pas allegro, these pas can be done with a beat; for example, saut de basque, which is very difficult, jeté en tournant with a beat, which is usually done by men, etc. Let us analyse a few examples.

To do assemblé with a beat from the right foot, we proceed as follows: if we open the right leg from the 5th position to the side, then on the return to the 5th position the right leg beats the left leg in front, opens again slightly in order to finish in the 5th position back. In order not to get a smear, it must be remembered that the legs beat with the calves, and that the leg should be opened before bringing it into 5th position.

Jeté with a beat from the right foot is done thus: the right leg thrust into 2nd position beats the left one in front, on the return it manages to open slightly, before you fall on it in demi-plié.

Small échappé with a beat from the right foot: after plié in 2nd position, on the return, beat with both legs calf on calf, right leg forward, open the legs slightly and fall into 5th position, right foot back.

Échappé battu can be done also in a more complicated manner: at the beginning during the jump from 5th position slightly open the legs, beat them with the right leg front and lower yourself into 2nd position in demi-plié; on the return to the 5th position, beat again with the right leg front, slightly open the legs and finish in 5th position back.

This échappé can be further elaborated thus: before opening the legs into 2nd position, do a beat the type of entrechat-quatre, and repeat it on the return from 2nd position into 5th position. In this kind of échappé one must do a high jump, almost like the one for a big échappé, although, in general, I recommend for entrechat-quatre a low jump. But the movements described are more complicated, and they demand more time, hence one could not make them during a low jump.

All these beats are done in this manner when moving backward; going forward, they are done the opposite way, i.e. the leg beats to the back and the final position is in front.

It is easier to begin the study of beats with échappé, and then work on assemblé and jeté.

ENTRECHATS

ROYAL

Stand in 5th position, right foot front; demi-plié, small jump, open both legs slightly; with the right leg in front, beat the calf of the left leg against the calf of the right leg, slightly open the legs to the side, and the right leg goes back into 5th position in demi-plié.

ENTRECHAT-QUATRE

5th position, right foot front; demi-plié, small jump, open the legs slightly and beat the calf of the left leg against the calf of the right leg which is at the back, slightly open legs to the sides and finish with right foot front in 5th position in demi-plié.

Entrechat-quatre is called thus, because the leg moves as if going through four lengths of a broken line: (1) opening, (2) beat back, (3) opening, (4) closing into 5th position front.

I repeat again, that the entire brilliance of this pas, its entire meaning, is to do it as close to the floor as possible, sharply opening and crossing the legs. It must be felt that the beat is done with both legs.

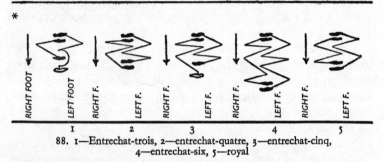

88. 1—Entrechat-trois, 2—entrechat-quatre, 3—entrechat-cinq, 4—entrechat-six, 5—royal

ENTRECHAT-SIX

5th position, right foot front; demi-plié, jump, during which open the legs, right leg beats back, open the legs to the sides, right leg beats front, open legs, and finish in 5th position right foot back.

This jump is done slightly higher. But even here one should not jump too high because during a high jump anybody will have time to do all the crossings. The brilliance of the performance can be shown only in a small jump, as this pas demands a great sharpness and speed.

ENTRECHAT-HUIT

Another opening and closing is added; hence, the right leg finishes front.

ENTRECHAT-TROIS

5th position, right foot front; demi-plié, small jump, legs open, right leg beats front, slightly opens and bends sur le cou-de-pied back, demi-plié on left leg. This entrechat as all odd ones finishes on one leg.

ENTRECHAT-CINQ

5th position, right foot front, demi-plié, small jump, during which the legs open, right leg beats back, legs open, right leg

* The white footmark indicates that the foot is raised sur le cou-de-pied.

Ed.

joins left one in front, and fall on right foot in demi-plié, left leg sur le cou-de-pied back.

ENTRECHAT-SEPT

5th position, right foot front; demi-plié, jump, open legs, right leg beats back, open legs, right leg beats front, open legs, legs join in the air (right one back), stop on right foot in demi-plié, left leg is in the air, or sur le cou-de-pied front, or in 2nd position at 45° or 90°, depending on how it was ordered. Entrechat-trois and entrechat-cinq may also be finished in various poses.

Entrechat-trois and entrechat-cinq we finish with the leg sur le cou-de-pied back. They may be done also to finish with the leg sur le cou-de-pied front. To do this, if the right leg was in front at the beginning, the legs open after the small jump, left leg beats on the calf back, slightly opens and is transferred front sur le cou-de-pied.

Entrechat-sept may be finished also in a different pose: front in effacé or croisé, or back in arabesque or attitude.

ENTRECHAT DE VOLÉE

Entrechat may be done not only from a jump on the spot, but also in a flight into any direction. The most convenient way to do it is from a glissade or coupé, but it may be practised also from 5th position.

89. Entrechat de volée

Entrechat-six de volée. 5th position, right foot front; demi-plié, left leg is thrust out to 90° to the side to 2nd position, jump, and you transfer with the entire body to that leg, doing meanwhile the necessary beats for entrechat-six. Finish in 5th position demi-plié, left foot front.

Entrechat-huit de volée is done the same way, except that the number of beats is respectively greater.

The corresponding position of the arms and turn of the head is used as in croisé. If the foot is sur le cou-de-pied, the arms are not high, one at 45° in 1st position, the other at the same height in 2nd position; if the leg is in the air at 90°, the arms acquire a pose as in attitude, arabesque, or forward, or in 2nd position at 90°, then one arm will be in 3rd position, the other— in 2nd position, depending on the required pose.

BRISÉ

There are two kinds of brisé: (1) those that end in 5th position, and (2) those that end on one foot dessus or dessous.

1. In order to begin the movement with the right foot, stand in 5th position, left foot front; demi-plié, right leg is thrust into the air with a gliding movement to the side, between points 2 and 3, then it beats front on left calf while left leg, with a jump, flies together with the entire body to the spot where the toe of right foot was when it was thrust out. Open legs and finish in 5th position, right leg back in demi-plié.

90. Brisé

This movement forward is very often used in the dance on the stage. Brisé back is used seldom, but we shall analyse it for the sake of completeness.

In order to move to the opposite side, stand in 5th position, left foot front; demi-plié, and slide it out to the side, between points 6 and 7; left leg beats the right calf back; with a jump travel in the same direction into which left leg moved, open legs and finish with left leg front in demi-plié, paying attention that the left leg is well turned out.

The directions, between points 2 and 3 for the movement forward, and between points 6 and 7 for the movement backward, must be rigidly enforced in order to produce a clean brisé. If one moves just diagonally, the brisé will have a careless, unfinished look, because the legs will not manage to cross over sufficiently and will only touch each other with the heels.

The arms in brisé take the following positions: during the upward flight the arms open to the side in the 2nd position, at the end of brisé forward the right arm is in 1st position and the left one in 2nd position. Only at the end the left arm can be in 1st position and the right one in 2nd. In both cases the arms should not be higher than 45°.

2. Brisé dessus. The movement begins in the following manner: 5th position, left foot front; demi-plié, right leg glides and is thrust out into 2nd position, beats front on left calf; open legs and lower yourself on right leg in demi-plié, left leg sur le cou-de-pied front.

91. Brisé dessus

It is customary to follow this by brisé dessous: left leg opens through 5th position into 2nd position, beats back of right calf; open legs and fall on left leg in demi-plié, raising right one sur le cou-de-pied back.

Brisé dessus is done moving forward, brisé dessous moving backward.

In brisé the body has a slight play. Namely, in brisé the body bends and unbends forward and backward depending on the

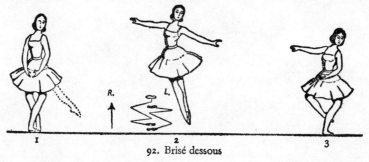

92. Brisé dessous

movement. In brisé dessus the body should be bent toward the right hip, in brisé dessous—to the left hip. The head moves in the same manner.

The right arm is bent, the left one opened to the side; at the moment of changing from one brisé to the other, the arms also change—the right arm opens, the left one bends when the head is bent to the left.

IX

POINT WORK

STRICTLY SPEAKING, pointe work is dancing on the extreme tips of all toes of the foot, the arch of which is extended.

There are various forms of pointes, however, and they depend on the construction of the foot of the dancer. The most comfortable for dancing on pointes is a foot the toes of which are of equal length, as if "chopped off", with a low arch and a solid, strong ankle.

The foot which we consider beautiful in everyday life, i.e. one with a high arch, a well-turned, slim ankle, correctly grouped toes, makes it difficult to execute movements on pointes, especially those movements which require jumps on pointes. However, even though such a foot cannot be placed on all toes, as required by the rules of ballet, it can be helped by diligent work toward a greater turn-out, so that the foot is supported by as many toes as possible, and does not rest with its full weight only on the big toe.

93. Pointes

In so far as pointes are concerned, the Italian technique has such unquestionable advantages that I subscribe to it without reservations. Cecchetti taught the dancer to rise on the pointes with a little spring, distinctly pushing off the floor. This manner develops a more elastic foot and teaches the concentration of balance of the body on one spot. The French manner of rising on the pointes smoothly from the very beginning of the training removes the possibility of technical perfection.

For the beginner it is difficult to rise on the pointes with a spring; for instance, to spring into 5th position on pointes. It would seem easier to rise on the pointe of one foot from a running start. Anybody can easily do that, but this manner of rising on the pointes is aimless. At the beginning one should carefully learn to rise correctly on the pointes of both feet in order fully to strengthen the tendons of the heels; a casually chosen manner of doing the movement will only make it more difficult for the pupil to learn the correct method.

Beginners should start the first study of pointes at the barre. Face the barre and put both hands on it so that the wrists touch, then begin by rising on the pointes in all positions, pushing off the floor with the heels before each movement. Under no circumstances should the beginner jump on to the pointes, before the tendons of the heels have been strengthened.

In centre practice the following order should be observed:

1. Temps levé on both feet. Stand in 1st position, demi-plié, push off with the heels, and with a little spring rise on the pointes; lower yourself in demi-plié, paying attention that the legs are fully turned out, and continue. The same movement is done in 2nd and 5th positions.

94. Sus-sous

If temps levé is done from 5th position into 5th position while moving with a small jump forward, back or to the side, the step is called sus-sous. At the instant of rising on the pointes the feet must be tightly closed, one behind the other, so that they make the impression of one foot. Properly executed, this step gives the dance a well-finished form.

2. Échappé on pointes. Demi-plié in 5th position, push off with the heels, and spring into 2nd position on pointes, lower yourself back into 5th position in demi-plié. One may finish in 5th position with a change of feet. In doing échappé in croisé and effacé, the movement is done from 5th position into 4th position.

95. Échappé (on pointes)

3. Glissade. Stand in 5th position, right foot front; demi-plié, slide the point of the right foot to the side and step out onto the pointe of this foot, and quickly bring the left foot, also on pointe, into 5th position. Lower into 5th position in demi-plié.

96. Glissade (on pointes)

4. Temps lié. Stand in 5th position, right foot front, both arms in 1st position; demi-plié, the point of the right foot glides forward into croisé, left leg remains in plié. Step onto the pointe of the right foot, changing left arm from 1st position up into 3rd position, the right arm to the side in 2nd position, and pull left leg, also on pointe, into 5th position back. Lower yourself into demi-plié (facing the audience) in 5th position, changing left arm to 1st position; slide the point of the right foot to the side into 2nd position, move left arm to the side and leave left leg in plié. Transfer the weight of the body to the right leg, onto the pointe, pull left leg, also on pointe, into 5th position front, changing right arm up into 3rd position. Lower yourself into 5th position in demi-plié and lower arms into preparatory position. Repeat the whole movement starting with the left foot. The same movement is also done backwards. The head moves in proper épaulement.

97. Temps lié (on pointes) 1st part

98. Temps lié (on pointes) 2nd part

5. Assemblé soutenu. Stand in 5th position, right foot front; do demi-plié and at the same time move right leg, sliding the point, to the side; pull the leg back into 5th position, jumping on the pointes of both feet, left foot front, pushing off well with the heel of the left foot. Lower yourself in demi-plié in 5th position. Do the same movement with the left foot front.

99. Assemblé soutenu   100. Jeté on pointes

6. Jeté on pointes. Stand in 5th position, demi-plié, move the point of the right foot on the floor to the side and to a height of

45°. Move right leg to back of the left and spring onto its pointe, at the same time raise left leg sur le cou-de-pied; lower yourself on the right leg in demi-plié, moving left leg to the side, and continue the movement with the other leg. In the same manner jeté on pointes is done forward and backwards, in croisé, effacé, and écarté. This step is preparatory to poses and movements on the pointe of one foot. In the more advanced classes we practice poses at 90°; we open the leg in a small développé in the desired direction, and rise on pointes in arabesque, attitude and other poses.

7. Sissonne simple. We begin to practice it facing the barre. Stand in 5th position, right foot front, demi-plié, spring up onto the pointe of left foot, raising right leg sur le cou-de-pied front and finishing in 5th position demi-plié. It can also be done this way: spring up onto the pointe of right foot, raising left leg sur le cou-de-pied back and finishing in 5th position. Another way is to change the leg, i.e. to place the raised leg back, or front.

101. Sissonne simple

Later sissonne simple is practised in the centre. Subsequently

102. Sissonne simple

113

when doing sissonne simple the leg may be raised higher, to the knee.

8. Sissonne ouverte. This movement is done on pointes from 5th position into all poses, beginning with the least difficult.

Demi-plié, spring onto pointe of one foot, opening the other leg with small développé to 45° front, in 2nd position, or back; finish by lowering yourself in demi-plié in 5th position. Later on we do grande sissonne. In it the leg opens to 90° in the same manner in all directions and poses.

103. Sissonne ouverte at 45° in 2nd position

Sissonne may be done in various poses and directions, for instance: sissonne from 5th position into 1st arabesque—after demi-plié, rise on pointes, springing to the side, into the pose; finish by lowering yourself into 5th position in demi-plié. All these sissonnes may be done in an unlimited number without changing the pose.

104. Sissonne in 1st arabesque

Lower yourself every time in demi-plié on the foot on which you are standing and repeat the rising movement, attention being paid that the leg in arabesque is kept at the proper height.

All the movements on pointes must always be connected with plié, and one must rise on pointes with a small spring.

114

Jumps on pointes should be done with a strongly held heel, keeping the arch and ankle tense and forcing out from them all softness. Jumps on pointes belong to one of the most difficult parts of point work, and their development demands great care.

Very often the tension in the ankle is transmitted to the body, and the body, too, becomes tense. This gives the dancer an inartistic appearance. In spite of the fact that the back should be held straight (as described in the chapter about balance), the arms and head must preserve their freedom of movement. Only then these jumps on points will produce the effect of being done with ease and absence of strain. Without this ease one cannot achieve artistry of the dance.

X

TURNS

Tour—is an old French term used in choreographic literature to designate a turn of the body on one leg. The term *pirouette* in reference to the practice of the female dance should be considered dead.[1] We will use the term *tours*. Male dancers still retain the term *pirouette* and use it to indicate multiple turns on one foot done on one spot, as for instance their *grande pirouette* in 2nd position at 90°. But we will use the word *tours*.

PREPARATION FOR STUDY

In the approach to the study of *tours* in their elementary form on half-toe I recommend the same gradation and attention as later, in the approach to the study of tours on pointes. One should not neglect the elementary exercises leading toward the aim of teaching the legs their proper position during all phases of the tour. Without this gradual study of all movements of the legs contained in the execution of the tour, the student may easily acquire a careless, approximate manner of execution. Just as strict should be the study of the correct participation of the arms in the execution of *tours*. The subsequent correction of a faulty manner in the execution of *tours* will require infinitely more time and effort than the painstaking work at the beginning. For this reason I recommend the following order for the study of *tours*, first on half-toe and then on pointes.

The teaching of children to turn their bodies serves as the most elementary, preparatory stage. In their exercises at the barre the following turns are used:

1. Turn on both feet.

In the more advanced classes:

2. Turn on one foot. (In every exercise when there is a need to change feet, one leg is raised quickly during the turn, and the movement continues with the other foot.)

3. Turn on the foot on which you stand and return to the original position.

---

[1] This practice is true of the Soviet ballet. In America and Western Europe, however, the term *pirouette* is considered good usage. In order to be as close to the original as possible, the author's preference for the use of the term *tour* has been retained in the translation. The reader will realize that he may substitute the word *pirouette* for *tour* without any change in the meaning of the term, except, of course, *tours chaînés*, *tours en l'air*, etc. (Translator).

The last-mentioned way is taught in advanced classes and is used in connection with battements tendus, petits battements sur le cou-de-pied, battements développés, etc.

All these movements are accompanied by a change of hands on the barre.

But all this only teaches the body to turn in general. We come closer to the actual teaching of tours in the following gradation.

We begin with turns on both feet and then continue with turns on one foot in the following order: (1) tours from dégagé,* (2) from 4th position, (3) from 5th position. After this, tours are done in attitude, arabesque, 2nd position, etc. After the study of tours on half-toe we continue to study them on pointe, maintaining the same gradation as in the preparatory exercises. Tours on pointe in attitude, arabesque and 2nd position are studied at the conclusion of the choreographic education.

Let us begin with simple turns in the centre—with turns on both feet. This movement belongs to the type of battement soutenu.

En dehors. From 5th position, right foot front, do demi-plié and at the same time draw the right leg to 2nd position, with extended toes on the floor; rise on half-toe, at the same time carrying right leg to 5th position back; turn to the right, en dehors, and conclude the movement with right leg front in 5th position. In this movement the arms play their part by helping the legs. At the beginning of the movement open the arms into 2nd position at half-height. Then, with an elastic movement join the arms below in the preparatory position, during the turn.

En dedans. From the same position, after demi-plié, draw the left leg to 2nd position and carry it to 5th position front, rising on half-toe and pulling in the leg. Then turn to the right (en dedans), accompanying it by the same movement of the arms, and finish right foot front. Attention must be paid, that the leg en dehors and en dedans does not describe an unnecessary arc on the floor, but returns from 2nd into 5th position in a straight line.

The next exercise is a change from one foot to the other with a half-turn on half-toe.

From 5th position right foot front, do demi-plié, dégagé with the right leg with extended toes on the floor into 2nd position; rise on half-toe of this foot, and draw to it the left leg into 5th position back with a half-turn en dedans; stop with the back to the audience, demi-plié, dégagé with the left leg into 2nd position, rise on the half-toe of the left leg, drawing the right one into 5th position front with a half-turn en dehors.

4   En dehors   3   2   En dedans   1

105. Change from one foot to the other in half-turn

The arms open into 2nd position at half-height during dégagé; during the turn they join in preparatory position with the same elastic movement as in the foregoing exercise.

The same kind of movement is jeté on half-toe making half-turns: with each change of legs move to the side, turning the body a half-turn, i.e. face—back—face—back, etc. The leg is drawn to the side, raising it every time to 45°. During dégagé into 2nd position with the right leg, the right arm is in 1st position, the left one in 2nd; during dégagé with the left leg, the left arm is in 1st position, the right one in 2nd.

4   3   2   1
two   one   two   one

106. Jeté on half-toe in half-turn

This movement teaches control, especially during the second turn, when the body is with its back to the audience. Attention must be paid to the turn-out of the knee of the leg on which the plié is done.

Having mastered the above-mentioned turns on half-toe, the student will easily continue to study the execution of them on pointes.

118

After these preparatory exercises one may begin to do tours in their simplest form.

TOURS FROM A PREPARATION, DÉGAGÉ

En dehors. Stand in 5th position, right foot front; demi-plié, dégagé with the left leg into 2nd position at 45°, draw it to the front of right leg on half-toe and turn on left foot, raising right one sur le cou-de-pied front. Fall on right leg in demi-plié, open left leg to the side in 45°, and continue the movement.

107. Turn from dégagé en dehors

Such tours can also be done diagonally. In these cases, when falling on the right leg, the left should be opened to the side diagonally.

The arms move the following way. Open the arms into 2nd position at half-height, at the instant of dégagé and during the tour join them in preparatory position. This movement of the arms gives the necessary force for the tour. During tours the arms should not be jerked sharply, this will only throw you off the spot.

En dedans. The following form is widely accepted: from 5th position, right foot front, demi-plié, dégagé with right leg into 2nd position at 45°, and step out on the half-toe of the same foot, turn en dedans, the left leg sur le cou-de-pied front; fall on left leg in demi-plié, the right sur le cou-de-pied front; and continue the movement. Subsequently these tours are studied diagonally, and later in a circle; then the left leg is sur le cou-de-pied back of the right one. At the beginning of the execution the body is turned effacé. During the tour the leg is kept sur le cou-de-pied back.

The arms move the same way they did in tours en dehors.

After these tours begins the study of tours from 4th position. Because of the preparation in 4th position these tours are easier achieved than the tours from 5th position which follow them.

108. Turn from dégagé en dedans

TOURS FROM 4TH POSITION

The study of these tours is preceded by preparatory exercises, during which all the movements comprising these tours are studied without turns. These movements should be taught in the beginners' classes.

En dehors. Stand in 4th position croisé, left foot front, demi-plié, push off the floor with *both* heels, which is very important, rise *high* on half-toe*of left foot, as if jumping on it with a short push (this manner is the manner of the Italian school, and it should be strictly adhered to, as it is of great help in the execution of tours); place right foot in a very close sur le cou-de-pied front just as sharply as it will have to be placed for the correct execution of tours. Hold this pose, trying to find in it a firm balance, and finish in demi-plié in 4th position, right foot back.

109. Turn en dehors from 4th position

The arms: during the first pose the right arm is stretched out in front, as if it were in 3rd *arabesque* (the body, too, has the direction of 3rd arabesque), the left arm is drawn to the side, the

120   *See Supplement, note 16.

wrists slightly raised. Rising on half-toe, join the arms in 1st position at 45°, keeping them rounded and strong. In the final pose just open the palms, leaving the arms in the same position.

With this exercise we prepare for tour en dehors. It also furnishes the preparation and the conclusion of the tour.

En dedans. Tours en dedans are studied in the same manner. The difference lies in the way the force for the tour is taken. In tours en dehors you push off with both feet from 4th position. In tours en dedans, you push off with the heel of the right foot, open the left leg into 2nd position at 45°, spring sharply on the half-toe of the right foot, drawing the left one closely sur le cou-de-pied front. When you are in 4th position, the right arm is bent in front of you in 1st position, the left one open in 2nd position; then both arms open into 2nd position during dégagé, and join at 45° during the tour; during the concluding pose in 4th position in demi-plié (left foot back) the arms remain in preparatory position, just slightly opened.

It should be said that this tour may also be finished with the left foot in 5th position front.

1	2	3	4

110. Turn en dedans from 4th position

When the students are well enough prepared, they are taught to make one turn, and later two and three. And then both the preparatory movements and the tours are taught on pointes. At the beginning of the study of turns, it must be remembered that the force for turns is furnished by the arms, never by the body, which must be immobile. It must also be remembered that the force is not taken with the shoulder, and the turn is done only around its axis.

TOURS FROM 5TH POSITION

Tours from 5th position are more complicated. Without the preparatory movement we had in 4th position, which furnished a convenient push, we must rely here mostly on the work of the arms.

We prepare for the study of these tours with the same kind of exercises.

En dehors. Stand in 5th position, right foot front; demi-plié, spring on half-toe of left foot with the same push-off as in the foregoing exercise, raising the right leg sur le cou-de-pied front.

111. Turn en dehors from 5th position

Right arm in 1st position, left one drawn to the side in 2nd position; during the tour it is the left arm that takes the force, at the moment of rising on half-toe, the arms join in 1st position at 45°, as in the first example. Finish the entire exercise in 5th position, right foot back, or in 4th position.

All this is done also with a turn. It should be mentioned that if many tours are done in succession, the right foot may be placed in 5th position front, and not back at the end of each tour.

En dedans. For a tour en dedans stand in 5th position, right foot front, demi-plié, spring on right foot, left one sur le cou-de-pied front. Lower into 5th position left foot front. Finishing in 5th position, one must restrain oneself so as to give a precise performance. The finish in 4th position is easier and does not require such precise restraint.

112. Turn en dedans from 5th position

In spite of the fact that the left leg is raised, the arms go through the same movements as in tours en dehors.*

TOURS IN ATTITUDE, ARABESQUE, AND IN OTHER POSES

We prepare for the study of these big tours with exercises on half-toe, similar to the preparation for the study of small tours, with the same preparatory poses.

En dehors. Let us take for the beginning the preparation for tours in attitude. The preparatory pose is 4th position, right foot back, right arm extended in front, left one in 2nd position. Demi-plié, rise on half-toe of left foot in the manner described above, assuming the pose attitude croisée. To finish, lower yourself onto the heel.

Then, make one *tour* on half-toe. If we use this *tour* in adagio, it is preferable to finish it on half-toe without a change of pose. It is necessary, as in the foregoing exercises, to push off in plié with both heels from 4th position, and, beginning the tour, to rise on the half-toe of the left foot with one push, establish the pose in a fleeting moment, and then make the turn, never disrupting the turned-out position of the left leg.

In this exercise it is very difficult to take force, especially for two or three tours. One must develop great deftness in the push of the heel, in the upward thrust of the hands which during the preparation are stretched out palms down. At the instant of rising for the tour, the wrists are gathered into the desired pose. All this gives force to the movement.

Tours in 3rd and 4th arabesques and à la seconde are done with the same preparation. The wrist of the right hand, thrust out at the beginning of the tour in the direction of the tour en dehors, helps to gain force. In the same manner can be done tours in développé, front effacé, i.e. during the tour the right leg is raised front, and you turn to the right.

En dedans. Force for tours en dedans is taken differently. This we learn during the preparatory exercises. Stand in preparation in 4th position, right foot back, left arm in 1st position, right arm drawn to the side. Rise on half-toe in attitude effacée, and in the same manner as in the foregoing exercise, lower yourself to the heel. When we begin to do the turn, we take force with the left arm, it is thrust into 2nd position, the right arm rises in attitude, the weight of the entire body is shifted to the supporting leg.

In the same manner are done tours in 1st and 2nd arabesques.

*See Supplement, note 17.   123

In these cases, the left arm opens into 1st or 2nd arabesque. The arm must be hard and sure as to the required direction, otherwise it may easily shake or jerk the body which is extended forward (see description of arabesques). For tours with the leg in développé forward in croisé, force is taken as for tours à la seconde, but during the tour the leg moves front into croisé, and the left arm passes through 2nd position.

TOURS À LA SECONDE AT 90°

For the tour à la seconde from 2nd position I prefer the Italian rather than the French way, because the Italian is sharper, more dynamic, and hence more modern.

113. Turn à la seconde at 90° from 2nd position

We begin to study it with the following preparatory exercise:
En dehors. Stand in 5th position, right foot front; demi-plié; rise on half-toe in 5th; arms front in 1st position; then open them into 2nd position and at the same time thrust the right leg with a grand battement into 2nd position at 90°, then both legs lower themselves into 2nd position on the floor in demi-plié, the right arm bends into 1st position; then the right leg is raised into 2nd

position with a swift, short thrust, the left leg rises on half-toe, the arms open into 2nd position. Stop with the left foot on half-toe and the right leg à la seconde at 90°.

The tour à la seconde is practised from plié in 2nd position. Attention should be paid that the heel of the left foot at the instant of the beginning of the tour does not turn in, but remains turned out as long as possible. This is the deciding factor in getting a well-executed tour à la seconde.

114. Preparation for turn sur le cou-de-pied from 2nd position

Force for the tour is taken by thrusting the right arm into 2nd position after the demi-plié in 2nd position. The shoulders must remain straight, the right shoulder should not be carried forward in an attempt to gain force.

En dedans. The preparation for the tour en dedans is the same as above up to the moment of the plié in 2nd position. After this the left leg is raised, and one should turn en dedans.

During the preparation the right arm is in 1st position, the left one opened in 2nd; force is taken with the right arm, never with the shoulder.

The French way differs from the above in that the right leg does a short développé à la seconde from the 5th position, after which comes plié in 2nd position, etc.

There exist also tours sur le cou-de-pied from 2nd position. They resemble those described above with the difference, however, that the right leg is opened to 45° and not to 90°, and that during the tour the right leg bends to the left leg sur le cou-de-pied. During the execution of the tour from this preparation the arms join in the preparatory position.

TOURS FROM 5TH POSITION (FROM A DEEP PLIÉ)

The manner of execution of tours in adagio from a deep plié in 5th position is entirely different. Beginning the plié, one should keep the heels on the floor as long as possible, but upon reaching the extreme point (i.e. lifting the heels from the floor) one should immediately extend the leg on which the tour is being done, and rise high on half-toe, keeping the back perfectly straight without any swaying. The arms, opened to the side in 2nd position at the beginning of the plié, should move smoothly down into preparatory position. At the instant of the rise the arms should remain immobile in that position.*

TOUR CHAÎNÉS

The French term is *tours chaînés déboulés*. I use both names because together they vividly characterize the nature of the movement. A chain of rolling balls—this is the description of the step, and it gives an accurate picture of it. Chaînés are done in very fast tempo, each turn in $\frac{1}{2}$ beats or $\frac{1}{4}$ beats. The movement goes forward diagonally from point 6 to point 2 of our diagram. Chaîné is very effective in the composition of a variation or other dance, and it is often used to finish a variation. Chaîné is executed in the following manner:

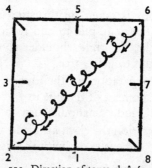

115. Direction of tours chaînés

When moving to the right, the turn is on the right leg, extended diagonally. At the end of the turn the left foot is placed front on the spot of the right one (never back). Give yourself a push by thrusting the right arm forward, then join the arms in front of you. At the beginning of the study of this turn, the movement of the arms is repeated with every circle. When the technique of the turn is mastered and the tempo is more and more accelerated, the dancer has no time to thrust the front arm out, and aids herself only with small movements of the arms in the same direction,

126   *See Supplement, note 18.

but without extending them too far from the body. In fast tempo, you give yourself a push to the right with the leg on the first turn and move on by impetus in the same direction, although the feet do not make a step but remain close to each other. The entire movement is aided by the arms (see above). In order to execute *chaînés* well, the dancer must possess great agility, must forcefully hold the back perfectly straight, and must never bend. Toward the end the movement transforms itself into a fast chain of turns which come to a close with an unexpected stop. One must stop perfectly motionless in a definite pose.

The virtuosity of this movement has achieved great heights, the tempos that are reached are breathtaking. *Chaînés* are done on half-toe and, later, on pointes.

It should be added that tours chaînés, jeté par terre, and others are often done in a circle around the entire stage.

TOURS EN L'AIR

These tours are the domain of the male dance, which I do not discuss here in general. Although the steps and the daily lessons are the same, the male dance requires more complicated movements because of the stronger physical development of the male dancers. Their work is easier because they do not dance on their pointes, a detail which takes up a great deal of the female dancer's energy and time. This energy and time the male dancer devotes to the elaboration of steps which are common to both sexes, but which, when executed by the male dancer, acquire a different character and a different grade of virtuosity. The male dancer also devotes less time to adagio. The female dancer needs adagio as an exercise to strengthen her body, which is by nature more flexible and weaker than the male body. At the same time this very flexibility of female dancer's body allows her to achieve those perfect lines of the well-developed dance which, with very few exceptions, are unachievable for the male dancer.

If I touch here upon tours en l'air it is because they can also be done by girls, and contemporary choreographers from time to time use these *tours* for girls.

Stand in 5th position, right foot front; *demi-plié* deeper than usual (but without lifting the heels from the floor), left arm opened to the side, right one front in 1st position. Push off with the heels, jump into the air, turn in the air, join the arms during the turn. Fall into 5th position in demi-plié, right foot back, arms closed in front. Attention should be paid that, in taking force, the right shoulder should not move forward before the jump, the body should remain perfectly en face.

GENERAL REMARKS ABOUT TOURS

The first condition of good tours is an absolutely straight, held-together body. One should not lose the spot of the finish, and should always "feel" the front so as not to get dizzy. For instance, if in the popular 32 fouettés the dancer should lose the spot in front of her and not face the front while doing plié, the fouettés would not come off.

Theoretically speaking, during tours as well as during all kinds of turns the head should face the audience as long as possible. But in tours the approach to this work of the head should be very careful. Attention should be paid to see that the head is not bent to the side and turned away from the axis around which the turn is executed. If you do not adhere to this, you will easily lose your balance. To gain the numerous multiple tours which are possible for the contemporary technique, this movement of the head should be used in moderation, stressing the movement only with your eyes, i.e. each time you face the audience look at it, and keep your eyes on it as long as possible.

In supported tours the male dancer must first of all stand well on his feet. An inexperienced partner involuntarily moves back his body at the beginning of the tours and bends forward only at the last tour, thus pushing his partner and throwing her off balance. He must stand perfectly straight, so that his partner may turn between the palms of his hands. The rest depends on the female dancer. If she turns well she should be left alone. If she does not turn well, the partner must help her turn with his hands.

There are several different kinds of pirouette in adagio with a partner. Tours are done from a preparation in 5th position on pointes, and force is taken in the following manner: remaining standing on the pointe of the left foot, bring out the right leg to croisé front, thrust it forcefully to the side, trying not to change the position of the hip (force is taken by the leg), bend it to the left knee front or back, and turn. The partner assists by holding the dancer at the waist, at the beginning slightly turning forward her right side, and at the swing slightly pushing with the left hand for the tour.

From the same preparation the dancer does tours holding on to the middle finger of the partner's right hand raised above her head. The dancer should hold on to the finger with the entire right hand, the partner assists her by turning his finger. But force is taken by the same strong swing of the leg. The deftness of the turns is concentrated in the experienced utilisation of the assistance of the partner's finger.

During the execution of all tours with a partner, the arms should be held not higher than 45°, closing them tightly, one over the other, in front. Another concluding remark: in tours en dehors, once a preparation is taken with the arm in front, the turn must be made from this preparation, and one should not swing the arm before the turn.*

*See Supplement, note 19.

XI

OTHER KINDS OF TURNS

TURNS IN ADAGIO

IN ADAGIO in the centre slow turns are done on the whole sole of the foot. Such turns are also used occasionally on the stage. These turns may be done in all positions: attitude, arabesque, 2nd position at 90°, développé front. This slow turn is achieved by slight movements of the heel in the required direction.

RENVERSÉ

Renversé, as the term implies, is the bending of the body during a turn. There are several forms of renversé, and it is one of the most complicated movements taught to the classical dancer. It is very difficult to describe, and nothing will take the place of a live example in the classroom. To demonstrate it properly the teacher himself must have a virtuoso's mastery of the dance.

We shall describe here the following forms of renversé:

Renversé en dehors. The movement begins with attitude croisée; demi-plié, the body bends slightly forward, stressing the movement by inclining the head, then rise on half-toe, at the same time centring the initiative of the movement in the back. The body is forcefully bent back at the very beginning of the turn en dehors. The turn is done by the body, the legs follow this movement at the last moment, doing pas de bourrée en dehors, when the body, which changed its centre of gravity, forces the legs, as it were, to make a step. The body forces the leg to move, the leg does not turn the body. For the effectiveness of this movement in $^3/_4$ time, on *one* the body bends and the turn begins with the rise on half-toe of the left foot, on *two* the body is held with the back to the audience, on the right leg, the back forcefully bent, the head in profile. This pose is held as long as possible, so that for the final part of the turn and for *pas de bourrée* there remains the shortest part of the third count of the bar.

The usual mistake of insufficiently brilliant dancers is to turn the body in renversé by the movement of the arms and steps of the feet, making the body follow the arms by their momentum. In such cases only the name of the movement remains. In addition to that the dancer loses self-control. The instant she repeats the movement several times in succession, she is carried to the side; trying to find her balance, she loses the rhythm, etc.

Renversé en dedans. This is a reverse movement, and its execution is much simpler and easier. Do a développé front croisé; the body bends forward and then does the same back bend and retardation in croisé, as in en dehors, into the pas de bourrée en dedans.

Renversé en écarté is done from the 4th arabesque. The right leg, from the 4th arabesque, bends into the position en tire-bouchon with the pointe to the knee of the supporting leg, which is on half-toe.[1] At the same time the body bends forcefully to the right, towards the knee of the supporting leg. The body turns en dedans, bends back, and at the same time the heel is placed quickly and firmly on the floor; the other leg opens in écarté back while the body bends to the left; stop firmly, and close into 5th position.

The arms join from the 4th arabesque with a forceful movement in preparatory position while the leg is en tire-bouchon, and simultaneously with the opening of the leg and the body, sharply open into 3rd position in écarté back. This movement, as well as the first form of renversé, presupposes a strongly developed body and a knowledge of how to take a movement with the back.

FOUETTÉ EN TOURNANT AT 45°

En dehors. It is done from demi-plié on the left leg, right leg at the same time opens to 2nd position to 45°; turn en dehors on left leg, during the tour swinging the right leg behind the calf, bring it quickly in front of the calf. The stop is again in demi-plié, opening the arms and the leg into 2nd position. During the movement of the leg into 2nd position, the arms also open into

[1] *En tire-bouchon* is the position of the leg raised to 90° and bent in the knee; the pointe of raised leg is pressed closely to the knee of the standing leg. A *pirouette* in this pose gives the impression of a corkscrew, hence the name.

2nd position. They close in preparatory position during the tour.

En dedans. It is done as above, but the leg moves first in front of the calf and later to back of it.

When fouettés en dehors are done successively a number of times, one should take something like a "swing". It may be done this way: do pas de bourrée en dedans and then begin fouettés. But this manner is not very dependable. It does not concentrate the balance of the body and may push the dancer off the spot. All depends on the individual qualifications of the body.

A more dependable way is the following: take a preparation in 4th position, spring on to the pointe, do one tour en dehors, and continue to turn, doing fouettés.*

GRAND FOUETTÉ

Although this kind of fouetté is done without a turn I describe it here together with the other fouettés.

The grand fouetté which we have worked out is somewhat different from the others. It contains certain elements from both the French and the Italian schools. Let us first analyse the Italian fouetté during which the body always remains en face.

En dehors. Pose croisé back with left leg. Coupé on left leg on half-toe, opening the arms into 2nd position during coupé; lower yourself on left leg in demi-plié, bend left arm in 1st position, carry right leg half-bent to 90° front, rise on half-toe of left leg, quickly do grand rond de jambe to the back with right leg, and finish in 3rd arabesque en face left leg in demi-plié. During grand rond de jambe the arms do the following port de bras: left arm is moved through 3rd position and in 2nd, while the right arm moves to 3rd position and through 1st position into 3rd arabesque, which it reaches at the instant the left leg is lowered in plié.

I shall now describe the fouetté which my students do, although in words it is practically impossible to describe the "method" by which the movement is taken and to reveal the correlation in time between the movements of the legs and the arms. This fouetté is governed by the arms; they give the movement to the entire body. To execute this fouetté on the stage without fear of losing balance, its entire structure must be fully understood and mastered.

Preparation, the same coupé, rising on half-toe of left leg, open arms into 2nd position; bend left arm to 1st position, demi-plié on left leg, turn body in effacé, carry right leg half-bent in effacé

*See Supplement, note 20.

to 45° front, bend body to the leg, pulling in the right side of the body and arching left side; rise on half-toe, carry leg through grand rond de jambe, and during its transfer, raise it, turn body to attitude effacée at 90° and higher, because with this swing one may give the greatest height; simultaneously, the left arm is raised to 3rd position and opened into 2nd position, the right arm goes up from 2nd position to 3rd position in pose effacé. Lower yourself in demi-plié.

117. Grand fouetté

The movement done this way acquires more plastic, classic forms, while the Italian fouetté is somewhat drier and more schematic, without transitional poses which soften croisé and effacé, etc.

En dedans. The right leg is half-bent behind in effacé at 45° and the body is bent to the leg; the right arm in 1st position, the left one open in 2nd. Rise on half-toe of left leg, carry right one through rond de jambe in the manner described en dehors, open leg to 90° front in effacé.

Right arm opens in 2nd position through preparatory, left one goes up into 3rd position. Lower yourself in demi-plié on left leg. This movement may also be done with a jump, following the same rules.

GRAND FOUETTÉ EN TOURNANT

En dedans. This kind is more often used than en dehors. Stand in pose croisé front, left leg front, coupé and demi-plié on left leg; spring onto half-toe and thrust out right leg into 2nd position to 90° with a grand battement jeté, opening arms into 2nd position. Lower yourself on left leg in demi-plié, turning en dedans, and gliding it on the floor close to the supporting leg, thrust right leg forward with a battement to 90° in the direction of point 6; rise on half-toe, bend body backward and complete the turn en dedans, holding the right leg at the same height, conclude the movement with a 3rd arabesque in demi-plié. It may also be finished in 1st arabesque.

When the leg moves forward, the arms move through preparatory position up into 3rd position, and finish in arabesque.

En dehors. Pose croisé, left leg back, coupé, demi-plié on left leg, thrust out right leg into 2nd position at 90°, rise on half-toe of left leg; open arms in 2nd position, thrust right leg through 1st position on the floor into 3rd arabesque in demi-plié, carrying the arms through the preparatory position also into 3rd arabesque. Turn en dehors on half-toe in croisé front at 90°, giving the arms the required pose.*

118. Grand fouetté en tournant

GRAND FOUETTÉ EN TOURNANT SAUTÉ

The same movement can be done with a jump. We begin the same way, and after demi-plié on the left leg, the right leg is thrust out into 2nd position; the left one tears itself away from the floor in a jump, while the right one is thrust out in the described manner. The turn is also done in the air, during the jump with the left leg.

*See Supplement, note 21.

SAMPLE LESSON

THE FOLLOWING is a sample lesson suitable for advanced classes. The entire lesson is given on half-toe.

EXERCISES AT THE BARRE

1. *Pliés.* In the five positions. Two bars of ⁴/₄.
1st bar—One slow plié.
2nd bar—One fast plié for half-bar. Rise on toes for half-bar.

2. *Battements tendus.* ⁴/₄ time. Eight bars.
Front.
1st bar—Four battements tendus, one to each beat, two with plié, two without plié.
2nd bar—1st beat—Two *battements tendus.*
        2nd beat—One *battements tendus* and rest.
        3rd beat—Four *battements tendus.*
        4th beat—Three *battements tendus* and rest.
Side.
3rd and 4th bars—Repeat the same to the side.
Back.
5th and 6th bars—Repeat to the back.
Side.
7th and 8th bars—Repeat again to the side.
Repeat these eight bars.
Execute the same exercise with the other foot.[1]

3. *Battements fondus and frappés* (combination). Eight bars ⁴/₄.
Front: one slow *fondu* for 2 beats, two fast ones taking 1 beat each.
To the side: the same.
Back: the same.
Again to the side: the same.
Two *frappés* slow, taking 1 beat each, three fast ones taking ¹/₂ beat each, rest on the fourth ¹/₂ beat. Do it four times.
Repeat the whole combination beginning to the back.
The same exercise with the other foot.

4. *Ronds de jambe.* Two bars of ⁴/₄.
Three fast *ronds de jambe par terre en dehors* each taking ¹/₂ beat; on

---

[1] Each movement of every exercise at the barre is always done from one foot and then from the other.

the fourth $^1/_2$ beat rise on half-toe, open leg in 2nd position. Three *ronds de jambe en l'air en dehors* each taking $^1/_2$ beat; rest on the fourth $^1/_2$ beat; four *ronds de jambe en l'air en dehors* each taking $^1/_2$ beat. *Plié sur le cou-de-pied* and *tour en dehors* for 2 beats.

Repeat entire figure *en dedans*.

The same exercise with the other foot.

5. *Battements battus and petits battements*. Eight bars of $^4/_4$.

Double *battement battu* with a rest in pose *effacé* front in *plié* four times, each taking 1 beat. During the next bar, *battements battus* are done successively with a rest on the fourth beat in pose *effacé* front in *plié*.

One *petit battement* with a rest in 2nd position four times, each taking 1 beat. One bar continuous *petits battements* with a rest in 2nd position in *plié* on the fourth beat.

One *petit battement* with a rest in pose *effacé* back in *plié* four times, each taking one beat. One bar continuous *petits battements* with a rest on the fourth beat in pose *effacé* back in *plié*. Repeat the described two bars of *petits battements* with a rest in 2nd position.

The same exercise with the other foot.

6. *Développé*. Two bars of $^4/_4$.

Extend the right leg forward with point on the floor, doing *demi-plié* with left leg (first beat), raise right leg to 90°, straightening the knee of the left leg (second beat), small, short *balancé* with the raised leg (third beat), carry the leg to 2nd position (fourth beat). Bend leg into knee (first beat), open in 2nd *arabesque* (second beat), rise on half-toe, drop back onto raised leg in *demi-plié* extending the left leg in front (third beat), rise on it quickly on half-toe, raising right leg in *attitude croisée* (fourth beat).

Do the entire combination in reverse order, from the back.

Third figure—in 2nd position, all poses to the side. The concluding pose will be in the first case *écarté* back, in the second case— *écarté* front.

The same exercies with the other foot.

7. *Grands battements jetés balancés*. One bar of $^4/_4$.

Prepare by extending the left leg behind. Through 1st position the leg is thrust front, then back (first and second beat), and twice through 1st position into 2nd (third and fourth beat).

The next time: throw the leg back, front, and into 1st position.

The same exercise with the other foot.

The body must balance as described in *battement balancé*.

I consider that these exercises fully develop the muscles and tendons, and think that artificial, unnatural ways of stretching which are practised sometimes at the barre (such as putting the leg on the barre) or in the centre are superfluous. I highly recommend the described exercises. The following method can also be of assistance:

Face the barre in 1st position, legs fully extended, hold on to the barre with both hands. Pull to the right without lifting the heels from the floor; return to the initial position and pull to the left. Repeat several times.

EXERCISES IN THE CENTRE

Realizing the shortness of the lesson I recommend the following order of exercises in the centre:

1. *Petit adagio*. Combine *plié* with various *développés* and *battements tendus*.

2. In the second *petit adagio* bring in combinations with *battements fondus* and *frappés*, and *ronds de jambe en l'air*.

3. *Grand adagio*, which contains the most difficult adagio movements for the given class.

4. For the beginning of *allegro* I try to give small jumps, i.e. low and simple ones.

5. *Allegro* with big steps.

6. For the first steps on *pointes* I select those which are done on both feet: *échappé* in 2nd position and then in 4th. This precaution is necessary because, although the students are warmed up, the new movements bring into play new muscles, and these should be prepared for the work.

7. In order to balance out all muscles and tendons which have been stimulated by the work, the lesson ends with small *changements de pieds*. To develop the flexibility of the body we do *port de bras*.

PETIT ADAGIO

1. Deep *plié* in 5th position, one and a half *tours en dehors sur le cou-de-pied*, stop in 1st *arabesque* with the back to the audience, continue the movement in the same direction and carry the leg forwards in *croisé*, look under right arm, raised to 3rd position; carry leg on the floor into 2nd *arabesque*, *plié* and do two *tours en dehors* in *attitude croisée*; finish with *renversé en dehors*. Two *battements tendus* back with left leg, two front with the right one, each taking 1 beat. Three fast *battements tendus* with the left leg, each taking $1/2$ beat and rest for $1/2$ beat. Repeat with the right leg. Six *battements tendus* to the side in 2nd position, each taking $1/2$ beat, flic-

flac *en dehors*, stop in 4th position, preparation, one or two *tours* on left leg *en dehors sur le cou-de-pied*.

2. Big *relevé en dehors* at 90° in 2nd position, carry leg on the floor into *attitude croisée*, *coupé* on right foot, four *ronds de jambe en l'air en dehors* with left leg, *plié* and *pas de bourrée en dehors*.

The same thing *en dedans*.

GRAND ADAGIO

Pose *croisé* back with left leg, *plié*, *coupé* on left foot and *ballonné* in *écarté* front finishing with right leg bent behind knee, extend it to *effacé* back, step onto it and do two *tours en dedans sur le cou-de-pied*, stop in *écarté* back with left leg, both arms in 3rd position; turn slowly and carry the opened leg into 1st *arabesque*, the body facing point 2, the arms opened in 2nd position through preparatory position are carried front with the wrists crossed. *Coupé* on left foot and *pas de ciseaux* (stop on right foot), turn to *effacé* front with the left leg, *chassé* in *effacé*, falling onto left leg in *plié*, after which change to the right leg, taking the pose *croisé* in *attitude*, turn quickly *en dehors*, stand on the left foot in 4th *arabesque*, *renversé* in *écarté* back, *pas de bourrée en dehors*, two *tours en dehors* from 4th position *sur le cou-de-pied*, *pas de bourrée en dehors* and *entrechat-six de volée* with the right leg.

ALLEGRO

1. Big *sissonne* forward in *croisé en tournant en dehors*, *assemblé* forward and *sissonne-soubresaut* in *attitude effacée* on right foot, carry left leg on the floor front, *glissade* with the right foot to the side, and *cabriole fermée* with the right leg in *effacé*.

2. (a) *Saut de basque* and *renversé sauté en dehors*; repeat; *sissonne tombée* forward in *effacé*, *cabriole* in 1st *arabesque*, *pas de bourrée*, *cabriole* in 4th *arabesque*, *sissonne tombée en tournant* (*en dehors*) in *croisé* front on right foot, *coupé* on left foot and *jeté fermé fondu* on right foot to the side in 2nd position.

(b) Four *sauts de basque* diagonally with arms in 3rd position, four *chaînés* diagonally to point 2, preparation in 4th position *croisé* and two *tours en dehors sur le cou-de-pied*; finish in 4th position.

3. Preparation *croisé* front with the left leg, *grande cabriole fermée* in *effacé* with the right leg and turn *en dedans* on pointes in 5th position. Repeat. *Sissonne tombé*: back in *croisé* from right leg, in *effacé* from left leg, with right leg *jeté en tournant en dehors* forward in *croisé*, *cabriole* into 4th *arabesque* and *pas de bourrée*. This combination may also be done in waltz-time.

1. Preparation *croisé* left foot back, *coupé* with left foot and on pointes *grand fouetté en dehors* on right foot, bend knee and, carrying right leg front *croisé*, rise twice on pointes *sissonne* into 3rd *arabesque* on right foot; *coupé* with left foot, *fouetté* on left foot *en dehors* to 45°, *pas de bourrée en dehors*, preparation in 4th position and two *tours sur le cou-de-pied en dedans* on right foot, stop in 5th position.

2. *Pas de chat* finishing on right knee, *développé* front on left foot on pointe *effacé*, immediately carry leg into *effacé* back without coming down from the pointe. *Pas de bourrée* (finish on right foot, left one *sur le cou-de-pied*), *fouetté en dedans* on right foot and *en dehors* on left one, stop in 5th position.

3. One *tour en dehors* on left foot four times (beginning each time with *dégagé* with the left leg) diagonally from point 6 to point 2, two *fouettés en dehors* and a third double *fouetté* also on the left foot. Stop in 4th position, right foot back.

SAMPLE LESSON
WITH MUSICAL ACCOMPANIMENT[1]
For senior and professional classes

EXERCISES AT THE BARRE

1. *Pliés.* In the five positions. Each set of *pliés* is done to two bars of $^4/_4$ time, first a *demi-plié* and then a *grand plié*. During the *demi-plié* the arm stays in 2nd position, head turned outward; the *grand plié* is accompanied by a lowering and raising of the arm simultaneously with the movement of the *plié*, the head anticipating the movement of the hand. Transition is made from one position to another by pointing the toes in a *dégagé*.

---

[1] All musical examples, with the exception of excerpts from the ballets of Tchaikovsky, Glazounoff and Minkus, are the working improvisations of S. S. Brodskaya.

2. *Battements tendus.* In combination with *plié* in 2nd position. Twenty-four bars of ²/₄.

Dégagé to 2nd position and open the arm before the music.

1st bar—Touch the floor twice with the heel, relaxing the instep and then strongly pointing the toes, ¹/₄ beat for each.

2nd bar—Deep *plié* in 2nd position, in two ¹/₄ beats, lowering and raising the arm.

3rd and 4th bars—Repeat this sequence.

5th, 6th, 7th and 8th bars—Eight *battements tendus*, ¹/₄ beat each.

8 bars—Repeat everything from the beginning.

8 bars—Thirty-two *battements tendus jetés*, ¹/₈ beat each.

The same is repeated with the other leg.

3. *Ronds de jambe par terre and grands ronds de jambe jetés.* Eight bars of ⁴/₄.

1st bar—Three *ronds de jambe par terre en dehors,* ¹/₈ beat each and on the fourth ¹/₈ stop with the toe pointed in front on the floor. Then bring the foot around *par terre* in *demi-plié* for two ¹/₄ beats.

2nd bar—Four *grands ronds de jambe jetés en dehors,* ¹/₄ beat each.

3rd bar—Three *ronds de jambe par terre,* ¹/₈ beat each and on the fourth ¹/₈ pause with the toe pointed on the floor in front. Then five *ronds de jambe par terre en dehors* in sixteenths and pause for three ¹/₁₆ beats.

4th bar—Four *grands ronds de jambe jetés en dehors,* ¹/₄ beat each. Repeat the whole exercise *en dedans* for four bars.[1]

The same is repeated with the other leg.

---

[1] In executing *ronds de jambe par terre* in rapid tempo the description on p. 39 of this book should be followed.

4. *Battements fondus and frappés.* Sixteen bars of ²/₄.

Dégagé to 2nd position and place foot pointed *sur le cou-de-pied*
front in *demi-plié*, before the music.

1st bar—*Battement fondu* forward, straightening on the beat for
one dotted ¹/₈ beat and *petit battement* beating front, back,
with the *demi-plié* for ¹/₁₆ beat. Another *battement fondu*
back, of the same type and in the same tempo, with the
petit battement beating back, front.

2nd bar—Repeat from the beginning.

3rd and 4th bars—Three *fondus* to 2nd position, ¹/₄ beat each, *plié*
on the left leg, and two quick *tours en dehors* from *fondu*
position, also for ¹/₄ beat.

5th and 6th bars—Eight *battements frappés*, ¹/₈ beat each.

7th and 8th bars—Eight double *frappés*, ¹/₈ beat each. The entire
combination is then repeated (eight bars), beginning to
the back, the final *tours* being executed *en dedans*.

5. *Ronds de jambe en l'air*. Four bars of ⁴/₄.

Begin by lifting the leg to 2nd position at hip level before
the music.

1st bar—Two *ronds de jambe en l'air en dehors*, ¹/₈ beat each, stopping in 2nd position. *Demi-plié* with the leg to the side in
2nd position on the third ¹/₈ beat, and rise to half-toe on
the fourth ¹/₈ beat. Two *ronds de jambe en l'air*, ¹/₈ beat each,
finishing in 5th position with *demi-plié*, right foot behind.
On the fourth ¹/₈ beat do a full turn on half-toe on both
feet *en dehors*.

2nd bar—From *demi-plié* in 5th position, one *tour sur le cou-de-pied
en dehors* on the first ¹/₄ beat, and repeat on the second ¹/₄
beat. On the third ¹/₄ beat do two *tours*; on the fourth
¹/₄ beat open the leg to the side at hip level.

3rd and 4th bars—Repeat everything *en dedans*.

6. *Petits battements*. Eight bars of ²/₄.

Dégagé to 2nd position and place foot pointed *sur le cou-de-pied
devant* before the music.

1st and 2nd bars—Six *petits battements*, ¹/₈ beat each, then on the
seventh ¹/₈ beat quickly change to the other foot with a
turn *en dehors* and on the eighth ¹/₈ beat pause.

3rd and 4th bars—Continue the exercise on the other foot and
return to the original position.

5th, 6th, 7th and 8th bars—Repeat everything with a turn *en
dedans* (4 bars).

7. *Battements developpés*. Eight bars of ⁴/₄.

1st bar—On the first ¹/₄ beat *developpé* forward and on the second
¹/₄ beat bend the leg to the knee. On the fifth ¹/₈ beat
developpé back and on the sixth ¹/₈ beat *demi-plié* on the
left leg. Then on the fourth ¹/₄ beat rise to half-toe.

2nd bar—On the first ¹/₄ beat turn on the left leg *en dehors* on
half-toe, right foot in front. On the second ¹/₄ beat turn
back again on half-toe, right foot in back. On the third
¹/₄ beat the leg slides quickly forward through first
position, ending the movement in *demi-plié* on the left foot.
This movement is executed like a *battement jeté balancé*,
with the body leaning back, and in the second case with
the body leaning forward. On the fourth ¹/₄ beat rise to
half-toe on the left foot, lifting up the right arm and looking under it.

3rd and 4th bars—The combination of movements to the first and
second bars is repeated but in reverse order, bending the
leg at the knee for the transition to each new figure.

145

5th bar—On the first $^1/_4$ beat *developpé* to 2nd position, and on the second $^1/_4$ beat bend the leg to the knee. On the fifth $^1/_8$ beat open the right leg to 2nd position, and on the sixth $^1/_8$ beat *demi-plié* on the left foot. Then on the fourth $^1/_4$ beat rise to half-toe.

6th bar—On the first $^1/_4$ beat quickly turn halfway *en dedans* changing feet, and open the other leg to 2nd position. On the second $^1/_4$ beat do this again and, on returning to the original position, open the right leg to 2nd position. On the third $^1/_4$ beat quickly brush the leg through 1st position and up the back of the leg to 2nd position, left leg in *demi-plié*. Then on the fourth $^1/_4$ beat rise to half-toe in *écarté* back.

7th and 8th bars—This combination of movements is repeated starting from the fifth bar in reverse order, i.e., doing the turns *en dehors* and ending *écarté* front.

8. *Grands battements jetés.* Eight bars of $^3/_8$.

Three *grands battements jetés* front, $^1/_8$ beat each; three *grands battements jetés* side, $^1/_8$ beat each; three *grands battements jetés* back, $^1/_8$ beat each; three *grands battements jetés* side, $^1/_8$ beat each. This combination is repeated during the next four bars. In the advanced and professional classes this exercise is done on half-toe at the barre and in the centre.

EXERCISES IN THE CENTRE

The first two combinations must be executed evenly and softly without the slightest hopping, for they take the place of the 1st adagio in the centre.

1. Sixteen bars of $^3/_4$.

Stand 5th position, *demi-plié* and *developpé* front with right leg *effacé* before the music.

4 bars—During the first bar step to high half-toe in 1st arabesque on the right foot.

During the second bar come down to *plié* in the same position.

During the third bar turn on right foot *en dedans* in 1st arabesque finishing in *effacé* forward on half-toe of the left foot, changing feet near the end of the turn.

During the fourth bar *plié* in this pose and continue. This should be done four times in a diagonal direction from point 6 to point 2 of our class plan. (see fig. 1, p.11) In the opposite direction it is done from point 4 to point 8.

2. Then this step is done in reverse, proceeding back from point 2 to point 6 and from point 8 to point 4 (also in 16 bars).

Before the music, stand 5th position, *demi-plié* and *developpé* back *effacé* with left foot.

4 bars—During the first bar step onto the left high half-toe opening the right foot to *effacé* forward.

During the second bar come to *plié* in the same pose.

During the third bar turn on right foot *en dehors* finishing in 2nd *arabesque* on high half-toe, changing feet near the end of the turn.

During the fourth bar *plié* in the same pose.

Repeat the same sequence four times to each side.

3. *Battements tendus*. Eight bars of $^4/_4$.

1st bar—Four *battements tendus* to the side, $^1/_4$ beat each, closing front first.

2nd bar—Six *battements tendus jetés* to the side, $^1/_8$ beat for each movement, closing the first one in 5th position front; on the seventh $^1/_8$ beat flic-flac *en tournant en dedans*, and on the eighth $^1/_8$ beat pause in 2nd position.

3rd bar—Four *battements tendus* to the side, $^1/_4$ beat each. The first *battement* closes in 5th position back.

4th bar—Six *battements tendus jetés* to the side, closing the first one in 5th position back—$^1/_8$ beat for each movement; on the seventh $^1/_8$ beat flic-flac *en tournant en dehors*, and on the eighth $^1/_8$ beat pause in 2nd position.

5th bar—One *tour en dehors* with preparation in 2nd position in $^4/_4$ time turning slowly. The slow turn for four $^1/_4$ beats serves for correct placement of the torso in learning *tours*.

6th bar—Two *tours en dehors* with preparation in 2nd position for two $^1/_4$ beats. Three *tours en dehors* with preparation in 2nd position for two $^1/_4$ beats.

7th bar—One *tour en dedans* on the right foot with preparation in 2nd position, turning slowly for four $^1/_4$ beats.

8th bar—Two *tours en dedans* with preparation in 2nd position for two $^1/_4$ beats. Three *tours en dedans* with preparation in

2nd position for two $\frac{1}{4}$ beats. The same is done with the
other foot.

4. *Battements fondus and frappés* (combined). Eight bars of $\frac{2}{4}$.
1st and 2nd bars—Three double *battements fondus* to the side in 2nd
     position, $\frac{1}{4}$ beat each, and two *tours en dehors sur le cou-de-
     pied* on $\frac{1}{4}$ beat.
3rd bar—Five *battements frappés*, $\frac{1}{16}$ beat each, and for three $\frac{1}{8}$
     beats pause at the side in 2nd position.
4th bar—Flic-flac *en dehors* finishing *effacé* front at 90° and pause in
     this position—two $\frac{1}{4}$ beats; repeat, turn and begin with
     left foot.
1st and 2nd bars—Three double *battements fondus* to the side in
     2nd position, $\frac{1}{4}$ beat each, and two *tours en dedans sur le
     cou-de-pied* for $\frac{1}{4}$ beat.
3rd bar—Eight *petits battements*, $\frac{1}{16}$ beat each, on two $\frac{1}{4}$ beats.
4th bar—Flic-flac *en dedans* finishing *attitude effacée* and stop in this
     position; two $\frac{1}{4}$ beats.

GRAND ADAGIO[1]

Four bars of $^4/_4$.

From 5th position in *demi-plié*, brush the right foot to the side in 2nd position up to a 45° angle and *pas de bourrée en tournant en dehors* finishing in 5th position *demi-plié*, right foot front; this movement is done before the first bar of music.

1st bar—On the first $^1/_4$ beat do two *tours sur le cou-de-pied en dedans* and on the second $^1/_4$ beat pause in *attitude effacée* with left foot raised. Then on the third $^1/_4$ beat make a half-turn *en dedans* to face corner 6 (see fig. 1). On the fourth $^1/_4$ beat, with a short brush along the floor through 1st position, bring the left leg forward to *croisé*.

2nd bar—Two *grands chassés* facing *croisé* back and stop in the direction of point 6 on the left foot in 3rd arabesque (in two $^1/_4$ beats). Quickly turn *en dehors* to *effacé* front and do two *grands chassés effacé* front, stopping in 1st *arabesque* on right foot (two $^1/_4$ beats).

3rd bar—Do *grand fouetté* twice *en dedans* with left foot to *attitude effacée*, two $^1/_4$ beats each.

4th bar—*Sissonne tombée croisé*, left foot back, on $^1/_4$ beat. *Sissonne tombée croisé*, right foot back, on $^1/_4$ beat, to a preparation in 4th position. Three *tours en dehors sur le cou-de-pied*, $^1/_4$ beat. Stop in 4th position, raising the arms to 3rd position, $^1/_4$ beat.

Andante. M. ♩=42

---

[1] The designation of groups of dance divisions with the musical term "adagio" does not necessarily require the musical tempo adagio; other slow tempi may be applied: andante, moderato etc.

ALLEGRO

1. Four bars of ²/₄.

1st bar—From fifth position *demi-plié*, do two *ronds de jambe en l'air sauté en dehors* with the right foot. Land facing back, having done a half-turn *en dehors*—all on first ¹/₄ beat. *Assemblé* right foot front.

2nd bar—Repeat the same with half-turn *en dehors* finishing facing front.

3rd bar—Double *rond de jambe en l'air sauté en dehors* twice, the first time from 5th position with a stop in 2nd position at a 45° angle (on first ¹/₄ beat). The second time, repeat with *temps levé* on the second ¹/₄ beat.

4th bar—*Pas de bourrée en dehors* finishing in 5th position, ¹/₄ beat. *Brisé* front to 5th position with left foot (second ¹/₄ beat). With the other foot the combination is done *en dedans* (also four bars). See below, number 2.

2. Four bars of ²/₄.

1st bar—From 5th position *démi-plié* do two *ronds de jambe en l'air sauté en dedans* with the left foot. Land facing back, having done a half-turn *en dedans* (first ¹/₄ beat). Finish with *assemblé* left foot back, on second ¹/₄ beat.

2nd bar—Repeat with half-turn finishing facing front.

3rd bar—Double *rond de jambe en l'air sauté en dedans* twice, the first time from 5th position, with a stop in 2nd position at 45° angle (on first ¹/₄ beat). Second time, repeat with *temps levé* (on second ¹/₄ beat).

4th bar—*Pas de bourrée en dedans* finishing in 5th position (on first ¹/₄ beat). *Brisé* back to 5th position with right foot (on second ¹/₄ beat).

3. *Free dance form execution.* Sixteen bars of ²/₄.

1st and 2nd bars—Fifth position, *demi-plié* and, beginning before the first bar on the off-beat, *glissade* in *écarté* with right foot front. Do a *grand jeté* to 1st *arabesque*.

3rd and 4th bars—*Glissade* in *écarté* left foot back and *grand jeté* back to *effacé* (opening right leg *effacé* forward).

5th and 6th bars—*Grand sissonne renversée en dehors* finishing in *demi-plié* on right foot, the left foot *sur le cou-de-pied* back.

7th and 8th bars—*Grand fouetté sauté en tournant en dedans* with left foot, finishing in 3rd *arabesque*.

9th and 10th bars—*Pas de bourrée en dedans* and *grand jeté* to *attitude effacé*.

11th and 12th bars—Repeat this figure again.

13th, 14th, 15th, and 16th bars—*Coupé* onto left foot and *tours chaînés en diagonale* to point 2 (see fig. 1). Repeat the whole combination starting with the other foot.

4. *Small beats.* Eight bars of $^2/_4$.
Executed in a strongly rhythmical manner.

1st bar—From 5th position, *entrechat-cinq*, left foot to the back, right arm in 1st position, left in 2nd (on first $^1/_4$ beat). *Pas de bourrée en dehors en tournant* to 5th position on the second $^1/_4$ beat. During the turn the arms close to preparatory position.

2nd bar—*Entrechat-cinq*, right foot to the back, left arm in 1st position, right arm in 2nd (on first $^1/_4$ beat). *Pas de bourrée en dehors en tournant* to 5th position on the second $^1/_4$ beat. During the turn the arms close to preparatory position.

3rd bar—*Entrechat-cinq*, right foot to the front, left arm in 1st position, right arm in 2nd (on first $^1/_4$ beat). *Pas de bourrée en dedans en tournant* to 5th position on the second $^1/_4$ beat. During the turn the arms close to preparatory position.

4th bar—Repeat the same thing with the other foot for two $^1/_4$ beats.

5th bar—Two *brisés* front with left foot, $^1/_4$ beat each, left arm in 1st position, right in 2nd position, but without showing tension. During the first *brisé* the palms are down and during the second the palms are up.

6th bar—Two *brisés* back with the right foot, $^1/_4$ beat each, right arm in 1st position, left in 2nd. Palms move as in preceding measure.

7th bar—*Glissade* with left foot to the side through 2nd position on the first $^1/_4$ beat. *Entrechat-six de volée* with left foot *écarté* forward. During jump arms are open in *écarté* position. Finish with left foot in 5th position front on the second ¹/₄ beat.

8th bar—Turn from 5th position *en dehors*, changing feet with both arms up, and end in 5th position, right foot front in a *demi-plié* on the second ¹/₄ beat.

5. *Big jumps*. Eight measures of ⁶/₈.

The direction is from point 6 to point 2 of our class plan, and the position is *croisé* back in *demi-plié* on the left foot before the music.

1st bar—*Jeté passé* back onto the right foot.

2nd bar—Repeat with left foot.

3rd bar—*Sissonne tombée effacé* forward with right foot. *Grand assemblé en tournant en dedans*, finishing left foot front in 5th position.

4th bar—*Petite sissonne tombée* back *croisé* with left foot and *cabriole fermée* at a 45° angle, the right foot front and facing point 8 (fig. 1).

5th bar—*Grand jeté* in *attitude croisée* with right foot, beginning its execution with a *coupé* onto the left foot.

6th bar—Repeat the same *grand jeté*.

7th bar—*Sissonne tombée* left foot forward in *effacé* and *grande cabriole* in 1st *arabesque* on left foot.

8th bar—Run, facing front, around to point 4, and from there, beginning with the 9th bar, repeat the entire combination starting with the opposite foot, moving from point 4 to point 8 of our class plan.

EXERCISES ON POINTE

1. Eight bars of $^2/_4$.

1st bar—Two *échappés* in 2nd position, changing feet, $^1/_4$ beat each.

2nd bar—Three *sus-sous* moving forward *croisé*, right foot in front, three $^1/_8$ beats. On the fourth $^1/_8$ beat stop in 5th position *demi-plié*. During the execution the palms open slightly to a small pose and the head turns to the right.

3rd bar—Two *échappés* in 2nd position with foot change, $^1/_4$ beat each.

4th bar—Three *sus-sous* moving backward *croisé*, left foot in back, three $^1/_8$ beats. On the fourth $^1/_8$ stop in 5th position *demi-plié*, the head leaning slightly to the left. Look over left shoulder to the back.

5th bar—Two *sissonnes simples* with the right and left foot, changing feet each time, $^1/_4$ beat each.

6th bar—Two *ronds de jambe en l'air en dehors* with the right foot, on the first $^1/_4$ beat. On the second $^1/_4$, close 5th position in *demi-plié*, left foot front.

7th bar—Four *sissonnes simples*, changing feet each time, $^1/_8$ beat each, moving back. The last one ends in 4th position as a preparation for *tours*.

8th bar—Two *tours en dehors sur le cou-de-pied*, on the first $^1/_4$ beat. Finish on the second $^1/_4$ beat in 4th position, both arms up. Look under arms to the left. Repeat with the other foot.

157

2. Eight bars of ³/₈.

1st bar—Fifth position, three *chassés croisé* forward with right foot on pointe in three ¹/₈ beats, finishing in 5th position in *demi-plié*. The right arm is raised at the beginning and gradually opens.

2nd bar—*Assemblé soutenu en tournant en dedans* with left foot, three ¹/₈ beats. Arms come together during the turn.

3rd bar—Three *chassés croisé* backward with left foot on pointe (three ¹/₈ beats), finishing in 5th position in *demi-plié*. The left arm, which was raised, gradually opens during the execution of the *chassés*.

4th bar—*Assemblé soutenu en tournant en dehors* with right foot, three ¹/₈ beats. Arms meet in the preparatory position.

5th, 6th, and 7th bars—*Pas couru* on pointe *en tournant en dedans*, left foot front, around the dancer's own axis for two ¹/₈ beats, left arm raised. On third ¹/₈ place right foot in front in 5th position, right arm in 1st position, the left arm in 2nd position. Repeat twice without coming off pointe in the direction of point 2 of our class plan.

8th bar—Then a short *pas de basque*, to 4th position as preparation for *tours*, and two *tours en dehors sur le cou-de-pied*, doing all this in three ¹/₈ beats.

3. Eight bars of ⁶/₈.

1st, 2nd, 3rd, and 4th bars—Do four *grands fouettés en dehors* in 2nd position at a 90° angle in six ¹/₈ beats each, finishing in *plié*, right foot at the knee.

5th bar—From this point, a half-turn is made on pointe in 1st *arabesque en dedans* on the right foot, ending in *demi-plié*. Then another half-turn in 1st *arabesque*, ending in *demi-plié*.

6th bar—Two *tours en dedans*, left foot in *tire-bouchon* ending on the left foot in *demi-plié*, the right foot *sur le cou-de-pied*.

7th bar—Step back on pointe six times, six $1/8$ beats, changing feet. Raise and gradually open arms at the same time.

8th bar—Preparation in 4th position, left foot front, and two *tours en dehors sur le cou-de-pied*. Finish in 4th position in *demi-plié*, right foot in back.

SUPPLEMENT

Note 1. The Author's Preface is called "Author's Preface to the Third Edition," and its first two paragraphs read as follows:

The third edition of my book *Basic Principles of Classical Ballet* contains several expanded and revised passages. I have also added a sample lesson with the appropriate music.

The French terminology accepted in classical ballet—as I have already indicated in all discussions of this theme—is unavoidable, being international. For us it is the same as Latin in medicine—it must be used. The Italian Cecchetti, teaching in England in the last years of his life, used this same terminology in a language foreign both to himself and to his pupils—in short, it is absolutely international and accepted by everyone. Nevertheless, now I have a slight reservation; not all our terms coincide with the terms accepted by the French. For many decades now our ballet has developed without direct connections with the French school. Many terms have gone out of use; some have been altered; lastly, new ones have been introduced by our State School. But all these are variants of one common international system of dance terminology.

Note 2. It is necessary to add that the achievement of full coordination of all movements of the human body in the dance exercise will enable the dancer later on to infuse ideas and moods into the movements, that is, to give them that expressiveness which is called *artistry*.

I do not treat of this matter extensively in the present manual, but I include it in my lessons, working it out in detail every day in my older classes and my most advanced classes.

Note 3. At this point I must make a remark of a general nature.

In the last few years a number of radical changes have been made in the distribution of class time at our school. These changes were called into being by new aims, which demand a broader mental outlook of future Soviet artists, versatility in the area of study of their speciality. While they are still students, we give them the opportunity to test their strength not only in lesson, but also in a little practical work—participation in ballets and productions performed at the school. The participants do not feel cut off from artistic life; from early experience they learn what they can and what they must get out of a lesson, and therefore they study consciously and seriously.

An important role is now being played by the general instruction now being given at our school. The general curriculum cannot be compared with that of the past, in both its general and its special subjects.

In my time character classes were practically never given; the work was learned from assorted dance numbers. The exercises for character ballets were worked out in detail in the 1920's by Alexander Shiryaev, who systematized the movements of character ballets and thereby enormously facilitated work in this area.

This is not to mention subjects like history of the theater, history of art, history of ballet, history of music and so on. In my time these subjects were not in the curriculum, since the theoretical preparation of dancers was not considered necessary.

To all the foregoing should be added the fact that for perfection in the choreographic art visual demonstrations are necessary. It is difficult to communicate our "mute" art accurately in manuals.

Time and again I have thought of Pushkin's lines:

> One foot touching the floor,
> With the other she slowly circles.

In our language, that is like performing a rond de jambe en l'air with one leg while standing on the toes of the other (that is, with the leg supported sharply on the tips of the toes). But perhaps it is not a rond de jambe en l'air that is being performed, but a grand rond de jambe at 90° traced by the leg—since the poem says "slowly circles." Further:

> And suddenly a leap, and suddenly she flies.

Where is she flying—upward or impetuously forward? It is beautifully described, but unfortunately it is difficult for us to depict these lines of Pushkin in terms of actual movements. Everything is in the realm of imagination.

In order to preserve all our achievements for posterity it is necessary to resort to the aid of the motion picture, which will be a great contribution to the immortalization of our art. The years are passing by, and we hope that our achievements, registered on film, will aid future generations to learn and perfect themselves.

In the not too distant future our first experience in this field will be shown to a wide public: pictures of the methodology of classical ballet at the Moscow and Leningrad Ballet Schools. This film will be a scientific aid in outlying districts as well. [At the present time this film is located at the Leningrad State Theater Museum (Russian editor's note).]

NOTE 4. When we speak of the position en face, we mean that the body remains straight, in contrast to épaulement, when the body turns.

Note 5. Before beginning to do the exercises at the barre, the arm opens into the 2nd position.

Note 6. When the name of a pas or pose is accompanied by the word *grand* (big), it means that in this pas or this pose the leg is lifted to a height of 90°.

Note 7. When placing a foot sur le cou-de-pied, from the very first steps it is necessary to be sure that the foot has not taken a doubled-up position, but that the above-mentioned rule is observed.

Note 8. The arms accompany the movement as follows: in the développé forward the arms are in 1st position; in the turning of the body the arms open into 2nd position. In the développé backward the same arm position is maintained.

Note 9. Those who belong to workshops of "plastic" dance, which was practiced on a particularly wide scale in the twenties under the influence of Isadora Duncan. The "plastic dancers," in opposition to classical ballet, championed barefoot dancing and "free" plasticity of movements representing a basic stylization of the pictures on ancient painted vases (Russian editor's note).

Note 10. In this case it is called pas de bourrée suivi.

Note 11. Flic-flac as a connecting movement may also occur when performing the adagio, sometimes, even, in a combined exercise, not from the 2nd position, but from any other position. Then its first movement should be executed in the direction in which the foot happens to be in the given case, without drawing it into 2nd position.

Note 12. When jeté en tournant is done finishing in attitude effacée, then the sissonne tombée is done again in effacé and the finish is in attitude effacée.

Very often in men's dancing jeté en tournant is done circling the stage, and if this method of performance is incorrectly learned, one's energy is excessive at the moment of leaping off. Perhaps this may even create an effect, but the absence of the necessary accent on the leg which fixes the attitude effacée position in which one finishes makes the performer unable to even out his body and finish the attitude properly.

Note 13. There is also a saut de basque in the opposite direction which is not used much in ballets; it is performed in the following manner: it differs from the previous description of saut de basque in that one leg, at the beginning, is bent in front of the knee of the supporting leg, and at the conclusion of the pas the other leg replaces it, also in front of the knee, then the legs will be in the opposite position. Stand in 5th position, right foot front. Do a coupé with the left leg, lifting it behind the knee and placing your right heel on the floor in demi-plié; move your left leg slightly to the side with walking movements; turn your back to the right; leap off in the same way, carefully throwing your right leg into 2nd position at 90°; turn with a jump (with outspread knees); transfer your weight to the leg, so that you do not finish in place at the time of the jump, but move on in the direction of the outthrown leg. When finishing, fall on the right foot in demi-plié, bending the left leg behind the knee of the supporting leg.

Note 14. When just beginning to learn ballonné, it is necessary to do it in place, without moving to the side; that is, from 5th position demi-plié glide the right foot sideways along the floor into 2nd position at 45 °, then jump with the left foot—and the withdrawn leg is bent sur le cou-de-pied, the left leg in demi-plié.

Note 15. This ["préparation dégagée" in Russian text] is an old-fashioned term seldom used now. I employ it only in my discussion of tours.

Note 16. When doing the exercise on half-toe, in order not to disturb the turn-out of the leg, which is so necessary in the classical exercise, one must not raise the heels high off the floor (see the accompanying figure). Only in a strenuous movement—for example, a tour in which you lift yourself off the floor by a strenuous push of the heel—is the leg raised high on half-toe. If turn-out is well developed on the low half-toe, it is less likely to be lost during greater efforts on the high half-toe.

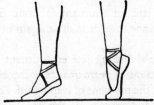

Low and high half-toe

Note 17. In the preparatory stages of learning the tour, hands in 1st position; but in a finished performance (a performance of two or more tours, especially with a partner), the arms must be held somewhat lower (see figs. 109 through 112).

Note 18. At the instant of the rise the arms take the same position as for the execution of tours from the 4th and 5th positions. (Replaces last sentence in first paragraph on p. 126.)

NOTE 19. At this point we have digressed a little from the theme of the book, since it is not our task to write about support by a partner.

NOTE 20. This pas, which up until quite recently seemed like the last word in difficulty and virtuosity, is now performed easily by good dancers.

NOTE 21. At the same time that fouetté at 45° is performed in one count, that is, on one quarter-beat, all varieties of grand fouetté are performed in two counts, that is, on two quarter-beats, one of which falls on a plié. Grand fouetté sauté is also done on two quarter-beats.

Grand fouetté en tournant is also done from 2nd position. In appearance this recalls fouetté at 45°, but it is performed in two counts. It should be begun along with the musical bar, throwing out the foot with a short movement into 2nd position at 90° on half-toe, opening the arms also to 2nd position. *On the first quarter-beat*, do a plié on the supporting leg; then do a tour, passing the foot behind and in front of the knee. The movement is ended *on the second quarter-beat* in plié, the foot in front of the knee (the arms simultaneously united in the preparatory position).

Like fouetté at 45°, this pas is done only on the toes, without jumping, and is performed by women.

INDEX